What People are Saying about
Feed a Starving Crowd

"This powerful, practical book is loaded with great ideas to help you sell more, faster and easier in any market."

> — **Brian Tracy – Author, Unlimited Sales Success**

"An amazing collection of marketing hacks and shortcuts. The only issue with this book is that after reading each page, you feel the itch to put it down and rush to your laptop to start executing on the many wonderful ideas you learn."

> — **Vishen Lakhiani, Founder & CEO, Mindvalley**

"Ditch your sales Prima Donnas, SEO gurus and thoughts of getting your MBA. Read this book, explode your revenue and reward yourself with a vacation."

> — **David Perry, Author of *Guerilla Marketing for Job Hunters***

"If you are looking for out of the box marketing techniques that really work, this book is a must-read."

> — **Benjamin Simkin, The $900 Million Dollar Marketer**

"Any one of the tested and proven strategies in this book will make you money. Taken as a whole they are a roadmap to the peak of your business potential."

— **Patrick Snow, International Best Selling Author of** *Creating Your Own Destiny* **and** *The Affluent Entrepreneur*

"In his book *Feed a Starving Crowd*, Robert gives some practical marketing tips that you you can apply immediately and get amazing results."

— **HC Joe Raymond, Speaker, Coach and Author of** *Embracing Change From The Inside Out*

"Robert has created a one stop shop for anybody looking to expand their influence, build their brand and sell any product. If you're going to be a marketing pro, start here!"

— **Michael Fulmore, Author of** *Unleashing Your Ambition*

"If you have ever felt lost in the online abyss when it comes to successfully marketing your product, this book will not only help you find your way, but will lead you to prosperity. Tried and true, the steps presented by Coorey to help your business become a success are the very same steps that brought about his financial triumph. There is a lot of advice out there, but his is the real deal."

— **Jennifer L. Tracy, Author of** *Sincerely, The Mentor*

"Robert has given marketing a makeover! This is a must-read for anyone trying to succeed in today's marketplace."

— **Sheila Paxton, International Speaker,** **Author of** *Getting Past Jaded*

"In this book, there are more than 200 unique marketing strategies, and 174 of these strategies require no advertising budget. If you are looking for ways to market without spending a lot of money, *Feed a Starving Crowd* is the book for you."

— **John Kremer, Author of** *1001 Ways to Market Your Books*

DEDICATION

ook is dedicated to my wife Dianna. I'm so blessed to have you
life. Thank you for your unwavering support and encourage-
More rough the many late nights I spent writing this book.

is also dedicated to my sons Pierre and Jacob. You are bun-
You're too young to read this book right now, but I can't
day when you pick it up and start reading it to me.

Rob

ACKNOWLEDGMENTS

Gary Ng: You're a legend and you have a big heart! You always put other people first. Thanks for believing in me and providing me with the greatest opportunities to make a difference in this world.

Lisa Jones: Thanks for supporting this book wholeheartedly and always encouraging me to dream bigger.

Patrick Snow: You are one of my favourite people to bounce ideas off, and every time I speak to you, I learn something new.

Graham van Dixhorn: I was trying to work out the title for this book for over six months, and you found it hiding in the first chapter. Amazing.

Shiloh Schroeder: I love the cover design you came up with. You knew exactly what I was looking for and exceeded my expectations.

Tyler Tichelaar: Best editor I've worked with. Your knowledge of what works and doesn't work in print is unmatched. Thank you for helping me make this a world class book.

Dino Bernardo, Adrian Ciaschetti, and Angela Yeow: It's a delight working with you in the office every day. Your commitment to excellence is phenomenal. Our insider jokes make each day go way too quickly!

My research team: Teresa Rodriguez, Jessica Benton, Victor Zhang, Daniel Han-Chen, Amitoze Singh, Jason Luo, Caesar Rosolen, and Stanford Lee. You guys are awesome. I couldn't have written this book without your help.

All the people I profiled for this book: Ben Simkin, Alexi Neocleous, Dr. Libby, Jon Benson, Joseph Assaf, John Kremer, Tzvi Balbin, Ewa Wysocka, Dane Maxwell and Andy Drish, Michael and Jodie Fox, Marilyne and Wyatt Woodsmall, Sam Cawthorn, Kerwin Rae, Dush Ramachandran, Eben Pagan, Jason Harris and Emily Shen. Your amazing achievements in life helped make this book.

5 REASONS TO READ THIS BOOK

(even if you don't like marketing)

1. Most people say you can't sell on social. They're wrong. I've got example after example of companies (including ones I've worked with) that are crushing it right now on Facebook and the other social networks. In this book, I reverse-engineer their success so you can see exactly how they've done it.

2. There are many marketing strategies in this book that require spending no money on advertising at all. For example, you will learn how a "small-time" promoter sells out high priced business events, how an "unknown" author launched a best-selling book on Amazon, and how a brand new e-commerce site completed a multi-million dollar launch. All of these strategies were successful without spending a single cent on advertising.

3. If you are fortunate enough to have an advertising budget (lucky you), you will learn how to squeeze every last dollar from that budget. Especially how to get the most hungry buyers hitting your website for the lowest price possible. In fact, when you finish reading Chapter 7, you will know how to get all the targeted traffic you can handle from 10 cents a click (hint: it's not Facebook ads or Google Adwords).

4. The majority of marketers are focusing on the big three social networks of Facebook, LinkedIn, and Twitter. There's a whole other world out there of little-known social networks that have so much traffic it's mind-blowing...and there is a very good chance your competitors are almost non-existent on these social networks. You will learn how to use Reddit, StumbleUpon, Slideshare, and Pinterest to reach hungry buyers rapidly with laser-targeted precision (hint: it doesn't involve "joining the conversation").

5. In this book, there are more than 200 unique marketing strategies, and 174 of these strategies require no advertising budget. If you just apply a few of these strategies, you can become an instant marketing genius, impress your peers, and gain respect for being a creative thinker.

FREE BOOK RESOURCES PAGE

Some of the content couldn't fit in these pages, so I have collated it all in a free book resources page!

Visit http://www.feedastarvingcrowd.com/resources to download:

- Screenshots of successful campaigns

- Actual results of high-performing marketing campaigns (including advertising copy, cost-per-clicks, and conversion rates)

- Webpage wireframes you can use for your own website that are proven to convert

- Diagrams and flow charts of automated marketing sequences that have been responsible for millions of dollars of sales

- Links to websites that have world class sales copywriting and are converting truckloads of visitors to buyers

- Interviews (media files and transcripts) with other marketing experts

- Links to online platforms where you can find other people to promote your product

To get all of this content, just go to
http://www.feedastarvingcrowd.com/resources

CONTENTS

INTRODUCTION
WHY YOU NEED THIS BOOK

"Movement is better than meditation."
— **Gary Halbert, world's best copywriter**

Have you ever read a great book, attended a great seminar, or learnt a great tip, and thought, "This sounds great"…but then you didn't take action on it?

We've all been there. Stop doing that!

People ask me how long it took me to write this book. My answer is fifteen years. This book is the culmination of fifteen years of testing, trying, implementing, failing, succeeding, and everything else in the middle.

I've worked in big business, small business, medium business, my own business, and everything else in between. I've used online marketing to sell investment properties worth hundreds of thousands of dollars, and I've used online marketing to sell baby toys for a few dollars each. I've sold photocopiers, enterprise software products, training courses, books—you name it, I've sold it online. Heck, I even sold 800 dog baths in twenty-four hours using email marketing (that was so much fun).

It doesn't matter which industry you're working in. Marketing is all about finding a starving crowd, and then feeding it what it wants.

Once I got 8,000 people registered for a webinar (and crashed the server). The world record is 10,899 attendees—so close! I was the co-founder of Punnky's World High-Five day with my E-Web Marketing colleagues. With no marketing budget, we organized for thousands of people across four continents to give one another high fives, and the Facebook following quickly grew to over 130,000 fans.

Right now, I'm at E-Web Marketing; we're a mid-sized online marketing agency, and officially, one of the best places to work in Australia. With table tennis, pool, trampolines, and an office dog, it's certainly a lot of fun! Channel Seven in Australia came to visit our Sydney office and filmed it—here's the link to see the clip online: http://www.feedastarvingcrowd.com/resources

How Did I Get Into Marketing?

Actually, my first marketing campaign was putting an advertisement in the Yellow Pages for a DJ service. That was fifteen years ago. I thought, "All of these ads in here for DJs are so boring! What if I put in an ad that is a little bit larger than the others, and made it sound more interesting?"

I spoke to the Yellow Pages sales rep and found out it would cost $1,000 to put the ad in the Yellow Pages.

Gulp.

$1,000!

I was charging $250 for a gig at the time.

So I worked out that all I had to do was sell four gigs from the Yellow Pages and I would get my investment back. Easy math.

I wrote the ad. The headline was "We play the music you want to hear." I had a little bit of text in there, something like "All music styles, amazing light shows, and fireworks."

Then I sent the ad copy to my friendly sales rep, paid my money, and waited.

Immediately after the ad went to press, I got my first call.

Caller: Hi, is this the DJ?

Me: Um, yeah.

Caller: Are you free on the 15th of October?

Me: Um, let me check my calendar…. (My calendar was blank, but I couldn't sound too available, right?)

Me: Yeah, October is a pretty busy month, but yeah, I'm free on that day.

Caller: Can I book you in?

Me: Yeah, all right.

Caller: What's your price?

Me: $250.

Caller: Okay. Here's the details of the party….

After that call, my life changed.

I had now realised the power of marketing. Think about what happened….

I wrote a few sentences on a piece of paper.

Someone I had never met before had read this ad.

He thought my ad was good, and he then called me.

I then got the gig.

How good is that!

Even to this day, I get really excited when people take an action as a result of a marketing campaign. Like today, for example. I wrote an email, sent it to my business partner's email list, and within minutes, we were making sales all around the world. It still blows my mind.

Anyhow, back to my DJ ad. Turns out there were a lot of people who liked the ad. I ended up doing hundreds of gigs all through my university studies, and it was a blast—all because of that ad I wrote and the $1,000 Yellow Pages investment.

As I've gone from spending just $1,000 on ads to millions of dollars, I've learnt that the most important secret to online success is not learning about the latest marketing fad or shiny new object. It's not creating the most expensive website or having the best produced video.

The most important secret to online success is taking action and actually trying stuff! Thomas J. Watson, founder of IBM, even knew this in the 1900s:

> Would you like me to give you a formula for...success? It's quite simple, really. Double your rate of failure. You're thinking of failure as the enemy of success. But it isn't at all...you can be discouraged by failure, or you can learn from it. So go ahead and make mistakes. Make all you can. Because, remember that's where you'll find success. On the far side of failure.

Nothing would make me more disappointed than if you read this book and took no action on what you learnt. Every strategy in this book has been tested and proven to be successful. There's no fluff or airy fairy theories or any rubbish like that. It's all tried, tested, and proven online marketing strategies that others have used and that have been successful. It's been a grueling process to get here. You're literally getting the cream of the crop, the best of the best marketing strategies that are working right now.

The easiest way to be successful is to model the success of others. And I've got it all laid out for you here in this book. All you need to do is read and apply.

Gary Halbert was the world's top copywriter. How did he get that title? He once wrote a direct mail letter called "Coat of Arms" that was mailed for more than thirty years…to more than 600,000,000 people! At one stage, Gary was banking tens of thousands of cheques every single day! Sadly, Gary passed away a few years ago, and he is sorely missed. I've always devoured any nuggets of wisdom I could learn from him. One thing Gary used to say was "You always accomplish more through movement than through meditation." I remember the story he told of when he went to Joe Polish's office and gave him some advice on a campaign. After looking through the results, Gary recommended to Joe that his team should follow up with phone calls after the mailing went out; then they would quadruple their sales. Joe thought this sounded good, but he never got around to it. I suppose it's never a fun thing to organise a tele-marketing campaign.

When Gary came back a month later, what was the first question he asked? Of course, it was, "How are those phone calls going?" Joe sheepishly talked around the question and made some sort of excuse. Gary then made Joe go to the bank and withdraw $21,000 in cash and bring it back to the office. (Side note: I don't know why

Gary chose $21,000, and not a nice round number of $20,000 or $25,000. Sadly, we'll never know.)

Anyway, Joe came back to the office with exactly $21,000 and put it on the table. Gary then picked up the money and started chucking it everywhere, screaming, "You might as well throw away this $1,000, you might as well throw away this $1,000.... Every day you sit here and don't make calls, you can throw away $1,000."

It's the same with this book. Within these pages, you are going to learn how businesses have made millions and millions of dollars online. And every day you don't implement the things you learn here, it's the same as you throwing away $1,000, and another $1,000, and another $1,000. That's why I've written this book to be more like a workbook than a novel. In each chapter, I share the freshest new strategies to feed your starving crowd, and there are exercises and questions for you to answer. The best way to get results from this book is to highlight and take notes in the book as you go along...and then take action!

All right. That's enough of a lecture.

One last thing before we get started—it's important that you go to the free book resources page (http://www.feedastarvingcrowd. com/resources) to download all of the supporting materials for this book. There's a stack-load of brilliant resources there for you to use as you read along in the book. Go there now, download the resources, and then come back.

All right, let's get into it!

1

FEEDING A "STARVING CROWD" AND A MOUTH WATERING MARKET FOR YOUR BUSINESS

"I'm always aware of who my core audiences are and I serve that niche."
— **Edward Burns, actor, film producer, and director**

No one in business ever wants to go hungry, right? Here's a tasty tale from my mentor Gary Halbert that you should never forget.

Halbert was running a direct marketing course and asked his students the following question: "If you and I both owned a hamburger stand and we were in a contest to see who could sell the most hamburgers, what advantages would you most like to have on your side to help you win?"

The students gave a range of answers. Some said they wanted better quality meat. Others wanted sesame seed buns. Some said they wanted the best location while others wanted the lowest prices.

After the students had listed their advantages, Halbert said he would happily give them all those advantages if he could have just one. With that advantage, he would wipe the floor with them.

What advantage did he want?

A starving crowd.

It can't be stressed enough: Before you start marketing your product, look for the starving crowds. They are crucial to your online success.

After all, there's no point making dinner if nobody's hungry.

So, how do you find a starving crowd? Let's take a look at a few case studies from some of the world's best known marketers—and one of my own too.

This first example from my own experience is a simple way to get started. Once you've read this story and done the Action Exercises below, I'll share some very advanced strategies for you to use—including exactly how Mindvalley found the starving crowd for its first million dollar launch!

The Quickest Ways To Find A "Starving Crowd" And The Best Markets To Enter

Assuming you're offering a service that people are hungry for, there'll be a starving crowd out there for you somewhere.

But how do you lead these crowds to come feast at your business banquet?

When I first began learning how to identify starving crowds, I needed to find a test business to apply what I'd learnt. One call to my father later and I'd found my guinea pig! I'd have full control over his business' website, could change the copy to suit, and would do whatever it took to make the site convert—hopefully, I'd remain on his Christmas card list.

My dad's business buys and sells excess stock—what better example of serving a starving crowd—and my first step was to put myself in the shoes of his potential customers.

I identified all the problems someone may face when he has excess stock he can't sell. I then wrote down all the questions someone looking to sell excess stock might want to ask my dad's business, including:

- How low do I need to go on price? (This really means: I'm afraid of losing too much money)

- How quickly will the stock sell? (This really means: I'm sick of seeing my warehouse full of old stock!)

- How discrete will the process be? (This really means: I don't want anyone to know about this; it's kind of embarrassing)

The list went on and on. When you sit and think about it, your potential customers have many unanswered questions that might lead them to your business.

The next stage was to create a list of phrases that potential customers would type into a search engine if they were looking to sell excess stock. I came up with a list of 127. I put the phrases into the Google keyword tool and identified twenty that had the highest volume and the lowest competition. I then checked out Google Trends to make sure there was still solid demand. And as you can see from the image below, there is consistent demand over a long period of time.

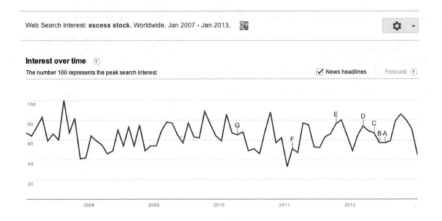

Web Search interest: **excess stock**. Worldwide, Jan 2007 - Jan 2013.

Interest over time
The number 100 represents the peak search interest

You can see that the demand for this search term has been quite consistent over many years, so it's a good market to go after.

With these twenty keywords, I performed some basic search engine optimisation for the site. It was soon ranking highly for these key search terms. Along with a homepage refresh (my brother built this for no charge—it's great having a web developer in the family) and a two-minute animated video (a few hundred dollars on oDesk), this process has generated over 1,000 solid leads into the business—a great result. In fact, there were so many leads at one stage that my poor dad started working early and finishing late just to keep up with demand!

And the best thing about it? We didn't spend a cent on advertising!

This means that the starving crowds are out there, but you're going to have to understand what they're hungry for.

So remember, if you don't send out the invitations, they're not going to come to dinner.

Action Exercise: Write down twenty keywords or phrases that people might type into Google if they're looking for your product.

1. _____	11. _____
2. _____	12. _____
3. _____	13. _____
4. _____	14. _____
5. _____	15. _____
6. _____	16. _____
7. _____	17. _____
8. _____	18. _____
9. _____	19. _____
10. _____	20. _____

Now go to your favourite keyword tool and find out which ten phrases have the highest volumes of searches—these are the keywords that will give you the starving crowds.

1. _____	6. _____
2. _____	7. _____
3. _____	8. _____
4. _____	9. _____
5. _____	10. _____

Advanced Strategies To Find Your Starving Crowd

People buy things for many reasons, and a lot of the time they "can't tell," "won't tell," or "don't tell" you these reasons. As a marketer, if you can uncover these reasons and use them in your marketing copy, you're well on the way to feeding your starving crowd.

My friend Alexi Neocleous, a legendary copywriter, taught me a lot about getting to the bottom of pain points to find the starving crowd. There's some fascinating stories about how to uncover these in Chapter 4—keep your eye out for them!

A "ninja" way to find a starving crowd is to look at relevant forums and find what people are complaining about. Look at Amazon book reviews. The reviews for the book give valuable clues for what people were looking for when buying the book.

Let me share the story of how I found a big pain point in Amazon. I was recently reading up on self-publishing and I came across a book called *APE: Author, Publisher, Entrepreneur—How to Publish a Book* by Guy Kawasaki.

Before buying the book, I was reading the reviews. (Don't we all?) One of the reviews was very detailed and gave the book only three stars. The reviewer was critical that the book didn't provide much help for unknown first-time authors.

A side note: In my opinion, three-star ratings are the best to use for market research. Anyone who gives a one-star or a five-star rating is biased. Three-stars seems to be the sweet spot where the reviewer has considered the book, enjoyed some parts of it, but has constructive criticism.

Back to the reviewer's comments. An "aha moment" came to me that help for unknown authors is a huge concern and pain point for anyone who is wanting to write a book from scratch and self-publish it. Authors want to learn how to sell the first 100 copies or so of their books. They've got no marketing budget, but they've got plenty of time, and they're not scared to do menial tasks to get their books out there. And they're passionate about their books—each one thinks his or her book is the best thing anyone has ever written. Fair enough; it probably is. Selling information products to bootstrapping authors is definitely feeding a starving crowd.

Guerilla Methods To Identify The Shortcomings In Your Competitors' Products

When online marketer Eben Pagan was single and looking for tips on how to meet "Miss Right," all of the books out there were teaching you what to do once you were already in a relationship. Eben's problem at the time was that he couldn't get a relationship happening in the first place! It's no good reading about how to have a better relationship if you don't have one, right? There was nothing out there that taught you how to get a date. That's why he wrote the book *Double Your Dating* and started his $100 million information marketing empire.

Dr. Libby (women's health expert) looked at all of the cookbooks on the bookshelves and found that there was a huge gap in the market for healthy recipes that were easy to prepare and tasted great! So she wrote *Dr. Libby's Real Food Chef*, which is about healthy food that tastes delicious. This book became a #1 bestseller for over twelve months straight, and there is now a Real Food Chef book series in production.

Action Exercise: Go right now to Amazon and search for the books relevant to your business and its niche. Out of the highest selling books, look at the three-star reviews. Find out what disappointed people in the book and write down the five most common complaints below. Here is your chance to serve your starving crowd.

1. _____

2. _____

3. _____

4. _____

5. _____

Very Quick Ways To Find Starving Crowds

A very quick way to find a starving crowd is to look at the Clickbank products for books in your niche. Clickbank is the world's largest marketplace of information products. When you look through the products in your niche, look for the ones with the highest gravity score—this is how many affiliates are promoting the product. The higher the gravity score, the more people who are promoting the book because it's a profitable adventure and the crowd is starving! My friend Andre Chaperon has done many, many sales on Clickbank, and his recommendation is to go for a gravity score greater than thirty.

Ewa Wysocka from Mindvalley goes to relevant Facebook groups and looks at comments and then looks at the profiles of people who commented to see how old they are, what they look like, do they have any kids, and what are their hobbies. From this data, she looks for commonalities across the board. She then puts all of the commonalities into a "customer avatar," or ideal client. This is the avatar Ewa used in Mindvalley's million dollar "unlimited abundance" launch:

- men and women

- 35+

- mostly professionals with small private practices or small business owners

- interested in personal growth and actively following blogs/newsletters on topics of meditation and energy healing

- had some successes in their careers but right now are not satisfied with their current income

- looking right now for a change or shift in their professional careers (Mindvalley launches this program always in the beginning of the year when people are in particular looking for a change)

- receptive to new personal growth concepts

Dr. Libby Weaver teamed up with us at E-Web Marketing to ramp up her online marketing. Before she creates a new product, she asks her existing customers what they would like to learn next. For her most recent book, *Beauty from the Inside Out,* Dr. Libby posted a Facebook message asking the fans what they would like to see in the book, and she got flooded with replies. Most interestingly, the most common requested topic was "How to remove dark circles under the eyes." And we built a lot of the campaign advertising around this single message. The book was a runaway success.

Out of all the people I've worked with, Dr. Libby knows her customers the best by far. She knows her clients better than they know themselves! This knowledge comes from her fifteen years of experience in the field and offering private consultations for over six years where women would share their deepest thoughts with her. Knowing your starving crowd so well means you are very well-positioned to understand what products would serve it.

Here is an excerpt from a chapter in her book *Rushing Woman's Syndrome* that shows just how well she knows her audience.

A Rushing Woman:

- Is so exhausted, particularly in the afternoon, a time when she is also more likely to feel like she cannot cope with her life... sugar, caffeine, or alcohol feel like the only options at this time

- Laughs less than she used to

- Finds it difficult to relax without wine

- Has a mental fuzziness/haze/brain fog that she only notices is there when she has a random day when it is not

- Beats herself up for not being a good enough wife/mother/ friend

- Is constantly looking for more ways to feel love or be praised, whether she can see this or not

- Feels anxious without her cell phone on her constantly...she can catch herself constantly pushing the refresh screen button thinking—"what if I miss an important text or phone call?" and takes her phone to the toilet for this reason

- Goes on holiday only to spend the majority of the time thinking she must unwind yet never actually resting... holidays simply become an extension of her usual life

- Tends to return from a break feeling even more exhausted than before she left

The power of understanding your starving crowd is amazing. A while back, I ran a list-building seminar in our office, and I invited the Dr. Libby team to attend. In one of the sessions, we were talking about their marketing plans and Dr. Libby's book *Rushing Woman's Syndrome* was mentioned. Out of the blue, one random woman in the audience said, "That's me!" Dr. Libby didn't even have to say what was in the book, what readers would learn, or why they needed it—that lady in the audience was sold at the title. That's why it's so powerful to know what your customers want and then deliver it to them.

The Three Schools Of Thought On "Product Naming" And The Pros And Cons Of Each

So now that you've found your starving crowd, it's time to think about what to name your offer.

I spoke briefly about Eben Pagan before. Eben is one of the world's best online marketers. He's created over 100 different information products and has generated over $100 million in online revenue in the last ten years. So it would be a good idea to take his advice on how to name a product, right?

Before Eben creates a new product, he looks at all of the pains and frustrations that the end-users experience and also their hopes and aspirations, and Eben names the product based on this, trying to make it sound like the ultimate benefit the person would like to experience (e.g. Double Your Dating). He also tries to use alliteration and rhyming. A lot of great brands use alliteration; for example: Coca-Cola, Kwik Kopy, Marilyn Manson.

Tim Ferriss promises a result in just four hours, so his books are named: *The 4-Hour Work Week, The 4-Hour Body, The 4-Hour Chef.* Tim Ferriss tests his names using Google AdWords to see which get the best click-through rates.

Before publishing this book, I had been thinking about the title for a good six months. And finally, I came up with three titles that I was happy with:

1. Feed a Starving Crowd

2. Instant Marketing Genius

3. Double Your Business Without Advertising

To decide, I ran a Facebook ads campaign for forty-eight hours, testing all the titles. I spent $20 per title to see what the results would be.

Feed a Starving Crowd was the clear winner, with the highest click-through rate. And that's my title! Check out the free book resources page to see my book title campaign results (and the titles that didn't make it) at http://www.feedastarvingcrowd.com/resources. I then repeated this process for the subtitle.

Action Exercise:

Step One: Write down all of the fears and frustrations your users might have before they take on your product/service, and the hopes and aspirations they are looking to fulfill after they take on your product service. If you're not sure...ask!

Step Two: Pick from the list you made the ones that seem the strongest and try to create a short list of product names based on them.

Step Three: Run a small Google AdWords or Facebook ads test to see what product name gets the best click-through rates—that's how you can tell which is your winner!

2

UNUSUAL WAYS TO LAUNCH
FAST AND CHEAP

"Behind every new product, there lies a dream."
— **Rolf Jensen**

When I joined E-Web Marketing, my first assignment was to fill up two seminars full of people interested in online marketing. One of the seminars was to be in Sydney, and the other was to be in Melbourne. The rooms could each hold 200 people. E-Web Marketing had booked the two rooms, but so far only two people had registered for the first seminar and ten people for the second seminar. Gulp.

Gary Ng (E-Web Marketing's CEO) asked me whether I thought I could fill up the rooms.

"Of course," I said.

Five minutes later, I realised the enormity of this task.

The first seminar was in Melbourne, starting in ten days.

And the clock was ticking.

How was I going to get the first 200 people to pay $47 and turn up for our seminar?

When your back is against the wall like this, you've got to roll up your sleeves and get your hands dirty. This seminar had to succeed!

The first thing I did was get a whiteboard and write up two numbers: Melbourne (2) and Sydney (10).

And then I thought, "It is going to be too hard to fill up Melbourne. For Sydney, I have three weeks so I think I have a better chance, but Melbourne is too hard."

I went to Gary and recommended we cancel Melbourne and just focus on Sydney.

Well. Was that a mistake or what?

"Melbourne's already paid for and it's an important first test so we can get Sydney right. If we give up in Melbourne, it's a domino effect. We're saying that failure is okay. Melbourne's going ahead. Do whatever you need to fill the room."

Phew. As Gene Kranz said in *Apollo 13*: "Failure is not an option."

I went back to my desk, took a deep breath, and pondered how I would do this.

All of these negative thoughts started coming up for me. Was I good enough to do this gig? Did I oversell myself? What if I failed?

At this time, I had a lightbulb go off in my head. I remembered a book I read a few years ago. This legendary book was written by Frank Pacetta, and it was called *Don't Fire Them, Fire Them Up*.

Essentially, the book was about sales management, and how Pacetta took over the worst performing district in Xerox and turned it into the best within twelve months, without firing any staff. The crux of the story was that he set higher expectations, didn't take any excuses, and celebrated every sale by ringing the bell.

If it worked for Pacetta in the early '90s, then it could work for me here.

There was no point being miserable anymore; I had two rooms to fill and not a lot of time to do it.

I added my email address to the form alert so I would get notified every time we made a sale. Anytime we made a sale, the "dong" was to be rung. No exceptions.

And then I thought, "What are all of the cheap, fast, and easy ways we can get people registered? How can we get this dong ringing quickly?"

We could email our customer list (even though nearly all of them were in Sydney, maybe they had friends in Melbourne).

All staff could write Facebook and LinkedIn posts to their connections—we had forty staff, so if everyone blasted at the same time, that could help, surely.

I found an affiliate broker who agreed to let us mail to its business database.

We had a friend at a widely read business blog, who agreed to write up an article about our event and share a link.

In short—we tried stuff! Lots of stuff. Many things we tried failed. The blog link sent no traffic and the social media posts were marginal. But the other tactics actually worked...and we got the rooms filled. Watson's theory of success rang true!

Now with a lot more experience, I would have filled the rooms a lot differently and with significantly less stress, but that's not the point.

The point is, even though we had to get down and dirty, we got the job done. The website wasn't pretty. The payments went through PayPal and we manually had to cross-check registrations to payments. The Google Analytics tracking was playing up.

I mean, there were so many mistakes, and if I did that today, I would be embarrassed, but you know what? We got the rooms filled.

That's my message for this chapter: There are many different ways to launch a campaign. You can do a webinar launch, you can run a four-video Jeff Walker style launch, you can launch through social media, you can launch using PR and traditional media. The sky is the limit. I'm including strategies and case studies of each of these launches below.

Again, the way you launch is not that important. What is most important is to have the mindset of "Failure is not an option" and do whatever it takes to be successful. Once you have that mindset, nothing can stop you.

How To Launch If You Have No Budget, No List, And No Product

So after Chapter 1, you have your niche selected and a name for your product. But if you've got no customer list, your product isn't built yet, and of course, there's no budget to promote it, so what should you do next?

I've been there and I've felt that pain. The good news is that I've discovered a way to pull this off. Although there is a caveat. This type of launch isn't going to be a million dollar launch, unfortunately! But at least you will make some revenue and validate that your product idea works. Then with the revenue you make, you can start to re-invest that budget and take it further.

This type of launch works best for information products, where you are sharing your expertise. I did this a while back when I launched our E-Web online training portal. We wondered whether if we put all of our training videos up in a portal, would there be a starving crowd to buy it?

Here are the steps I took:

1. I compiled a list of everyone who had subscribed to our email newsletter. (Note: If you don't have a list, go to your LinkedIn and export anyone who looks like he or she could be inter-

ested. Also look through any old business cards you have, your Facebook friends, your mobile phone contacts, anyone who could be interested. Don't be shy here; you need to scrape and scrounge every possible chance for making a sale! It's perfectly okay to email your personal contacts once to let them know what you're up to. Any more than that gets annoying.)

2. I secured the right to blast an affiliate's email database to get more signups. If you can find someone who has an email list with your ideal types of clients, then you can also do this. See Chapter 6 for a whole chapter devoted to this topic.

3. I then emailed people from these two sources with the pre-launch offer, inviting them to a free webinar. The webinar is all good content for fifty-five minutes and a five-minute offer at the end. The offer I made was a five-week online training course, in which I deliver five live webinars with Q&A at the end. The price I charged was $997. They would also get full access to any future training videos.

Five hundred people attended and eight people bought. Not the greatest conversion rate in the world, but not the worst either.

I spent about forty hours on this whole project, including delivering the training. Total revenue was $7,976, which is $199/hour. Not bad. Again, could be better but not the worst either.

The good news is I recorded the five training calls, so now I can also give them away as a bonus when we do other launches.

As you can see, this was a very valid strategy and an easy way to get started.

Since running this first webinar, I've gone on to run dozens of webinars, and I've sold products by the bucket load through webinars. In fact, for one client's webinar, I managed to get 8,000 people registered—enough people to fill up a stadium! It was so many people that it actually crashed the server—some would say that's a high quality problem.

Action Exercise: Are there any new products/services you'd like to try to see whether anyone will buy ? List your top five ideas below.

1. _____

2. _____

3. _____

4. _____

5. _____

If you don't have a list already, find at least 200 people and add them to your list. You can use your address book and your Facebook, LinkedIn, and Twitter contacts. Now set up a webinar and invite your list to come!

How A Business Coach Sold-Out A Multi-Million Dollar Training Event Without Any Paid Advertising

Eben Pagan recently executed one of the best launches I have seen. He sold out a $10,000 ticket training event using just online marketing and without any paid advertising. Most people struggle to fill up any type of paid event without a telephone sales team. Eben filled a room of 400 people. Pretty amazing! Here's how he did it:

Over a two-week period, he blasted out four videos (one every four days). All of the email marketing goes to one mega launch page (http://accelerate.splashthat.com/).

In Video 1, Eben shared some great content about productivity. He then encouraged viewers to download a PDF report and some exercises about productivity. And here's the brilliant part. The hardest thing to do with these launches is to keep people engaged. Eben achieved this engagement by creating a competition. The competition gave viewers the chance to win a MacBook Pro, MacBook Air, or an iPad mini, just by submitting the exercises through social media. This idea was brilliant for three reasons:

1. People actually stayed engaged through the launch to see whether they had won.

2. People actually did the work, got a good result in advance, and were more likely to think Eben was a brilliant teacher so they wanted to register for the event.

3. People were sharing their homework on social media and it got spread out to all of their fans—more social proof and virality.

Eben emailed the list three times about Video 1—one initial email and two reminder emails to participate. In fact, he sent out around thirty emails promoting this launch to his list. Some may say that is excessive, but others would say, "Model what works!"

Then came Video 2, which revealed content about marketing. Again, Eben provided a PDF report, exercises, and a competition. This time, he sent one email to start and one reminder email.

The topic of Video 3 was hiring superstars and "A-grade" players. Again, the report and exercises and competition formula. Again, one email to start and two reminder emails.

And finally, we get to Video 4, which was a sales video, followed by a live webinar. There were three emails to remind about the webinar and one email to launch the "early bird" cart. The sales video went for one hour and went into immense detail about what you would get at the training event.

If you were on Eben's email list at the time, you couldn't complain about not knowing the event was coming.... He sent twelve more follow-up emails over nine days. The "Early bird" cart to register for the training event was open for seven days and offered 50 percent off the training. An early bird cart is a great way to give a discount without it seeming to devalue your offering.

How Eben Was Able To Get Massive Affiliates On Board

Eben also got massive affiliates on board. He's been in the industry a long time and has great personal connections. Another reason he got a lot of affiliates on board is because of hard work! His affiliate managers attend many marketing conferences, and they network well and make new connections. He built a dedicated affiliate site and gave his affiliates all the details (swipe copy to send to their list, dates and times for each blast).

To get people on board as an affiliate, it's very helpful if you can demonstrate past performance of product launches and if you have awesome prizes. Prizes make affiliates fight hard to sell your product. Eben's top five affiliates got a MacBook Pro. The top ten got iPads. All along, Eben kept the leaderboard tally public, so as the affiliates went along, they had a push to get them a top spot.

The top person got a $50,000 cash prize. The second person got a $25,000 cash prize. And here's the kicker—anyone who mailed all three mailings for pre-launch videos got double the prize—that's $100,000 as the top prize. There were two contests: a lead contest and a sales contest. One contest to see how many leads you could deliver, and one contest to see how many sales you could deliver.

With all of these incentives, it's no wonder the affiliates were so hungry to mail.

Action exercise: Write down the names of twenty potential affiliates for what you sell. The best way to think of who is a good match is any person or company who is also selling to your market. For example, for Eben's seminar about business, any company that sells business advice to its customers is a natural affiliate.

1. _____   11. _____

2. _____   12. _____

3. _____   13. _____

4. _____   14. _____

5. _____   15. _____

6. _____   16. _____

7. _____   17. _____

8. _____   18. _____

9. _____   19. _____

10. _____   20. _____

In Chapter 6, I will show you how to contact these affiliates in the best way possible, but for now, just write down your list.

How An Online Membership Site Did $100,000 Launch Through Facebook Posts Only

This is a great story about two young guys, Jared Hopping (twenty-three years old) and Brett Cosgriff (twenty-five years old). These guys had an uncanny knack of being brilliant tipsters for sporting events. As an example, they were able to pick the most valuable player for the

Australian Rules football grand finale a full *two* weeks before the game. They created a Facebook page and got 9,000 Likes in just two weeks.

Sensing an opportunity here, the two men then contacted entrepreneurs Nathan Rothschild and Jonathan Weinstock to turn their sports tipping skills into a proper business. And "MVP Genius" was born.

For two weeks before the launch of the business, they continually posted Facebook messages with great sporting tips and general hype-building. And then it came to launch day. Would this business be a "green-light" or would it be a whimpering failure? People loved their free tips, but would they be prepared to pay for them? Only one way to find out.

They hit the "go" button on launch. And held their breath.

In the first forty-five minutes, they sold seventeen annual packages at $699 each. In the first two days, they sold $50,000 of advice, and by the end of the launch, they hit $100,000 in revenue. Not bad for a few Facebook posts!

Note—their first website was awful! And they still managed to hit $100,000 in revenue. Goes to show you—if you're selling something that people want, you can do well, in spite of having an ugly website.

This was a great campaign that demonstrates how to feed a starving crowd through social media.

PR Launch: How A Brand New Ecommerce Site Got 2.6 Million Visitors In 24 Hours Using Only PR And No Advertising

Imagine getting 2.6 million visitors to your site in twenty-four hours. Actually, those numbers are so staggering they're hard to fathom. It's like all the adults in a major city going to your website at the same time.

That's what happened to Click Frenzy: Australia's answer to online shopping. The twenty-four-hour online sales event first took place on November 20, 2012. Click Frenzy gained an extraordinary level of attention across all facets of media—television, radio, print, and online publications—both in Australia and overseas.

According to Media Monitors, the campaign received 900+ mentions in the media. Every major newspaper, TV station, radio station, and online business blog reported the story.

Initially, the media hype centered on the new "mega sale" concept, which had never been seen in the Australian online shopping landscape. Click Frenzy is modeled closely on the U.S.'s successful Cyber Monday event, which was launched in 2006 by the American ecommerce industry as a way for online retailers to capitalise on the Thanksgiving holiday Black Friday phenomenon. Black Friday (following the Thanksgiving Day feast on the fourth Thursday in November) is the biggest retail sales day on the U.S. calendar. Now, Cyber Monday (following that weekend) is the biggest online sales event in the U.S., growing explosively every year.

The consumer hunger for Click Frenzy was so intense it caused website crashes for some of the participating retailers, including the Click Frenzy site. How unlucky is that? So many people hit the website that it crashed....

The site infrastructure was unable to handle the high volume of site visitors logging into the site at the same time. Despite the technical glitches, though, many of the retailers participating in the event overcame the initial performance woes and registered record online sales figures. The below table quantifies Click Frenzy's staggering traffic volumes during the initial twenty-four-hour period.

SOME NUMBERS BEHIND THE EVENT:

TOTAL SITE VISITS: 2.6 million

UNIQUE VISITS: 1.6 million

PAGE VIEWS: 22 million+

AVERAGE SITE DURATION: 7.45 mins

BOUNCE RATE: 22 percent

Deconstructing The PR Campaign

The Click Frenzy PR campaign really took hold when the Australian mainstream television and print media got behind the story. Channel Nine's *A Current Affair* was the first to include an exclusive feature on Click Frenzy. An "exclusive" is always attractive to journalists because they know they're being given unique, juicy content that won't be available anywhere else. While other media publications had been covering the story, *A Current Affair* was given access to the backend site before the event began, so it was able to share with its viewers "sneak peek" deals in readiness for the sales event. A similar strategy was used with newspaper and online publications across Australia with a separate array of deals shared. The producers and editors of these news outlets recognised the Australian consumer's appetite for a bargain.

The production of these media features was the tip of the iceberg. What followed was media publicity on steroids. Just about every media outlet in Australia was covering the story, from technology outlets to niche marketing and business news companies; they all had their angles on Click Frenzy. Some marvelled at the concept, while other "experts" predicted the technology hitches. Press releases were sent out to the huge media database that continued to grow as attention for the event did. A substantial media contact list had been created by the PR manager in the lead-up to the event, and it continued to grow as more media outlets contacted the company. The Click Frenzy website also included a press section where media kits and contact details were accessible for journalists and editors.

The anatomy of the press releases included background information on the Click Frenzy idea—inspiration, goals, and targets, as well as testimonials from participating retailers and business leaders in the retail and ecommerce space. Participating retailers or "ambassadors" also took part in the media stir, agreeing to be profiled in media releases and featured in the news programs. These companies gained a lot of brand exposure in the process. Having well-known, household retail companies acting as advocates also did a lot for the Click Frenzy brand credibility.

Post-event press releases included facts and figures from the sales event, as well as the results from some of the participating retailers. When the technology glitches occurred, Click Frenzy had to issue formal press statements explaining the situation, while not having the complete answers yet itself. The social media fallout was also severe.

Bursting The PR Bubble

Reputations can be fostered and burst in a moment's time. Facebook and Twitter can be a great form of promotion and engagement, but these channels can also become a platform for word-of-mouth steroids, with negative commentary having the potential to spiral into an out-of-control viral attack that can tarnish brand reputations. Click Frenzy was no different.

When the site crashed during the first sales event, consumers took to the social media channels and forums in anger. The social pages were full of negative commentary, and there were even social "trolls" out looking for an opportunity to attack. Click Frenzy personnel tried their best to monitor the channels and respond to the complaints. There were also some instances where content had to be pulled from the pages because it was too offensive.

Personally, I don't know why people go to so much trouble to write negative comments. They're better off investing that time and energy into something better.... But regardless, in the age of social media, businesses need to be prepared for this kind of response.

Anyway, the good news for Click Frenzy is that it now has a massive database of users interested in deals, and it's run a number of events since then with the servers holding up well.

And the good news for you is that if your idea is interesting enough, the media has the potential to send a "frenzy" of traffic to your site.

Click Frenzy was a phenomenal success in terms of the PR element. Spurred on by the Australian public's hungry appetite for online shopping, it proved the power that media has in creating interest and controversy. The media hype surrounding the event was amazing, and it exceeded the organiser's expectations like nothing else. For an event that had been previously unknown, Click Frenzy shifted to become an Australian household name. There's no denying the PR traction worked.

Action exercise: Are there any media outlets that would be a natural fit for what you sell? Create a list of ten of them. Then put together a short pitch and send it to the relevant journalist at each of the ten media outlets you've chosen. See what the journalists' feedback is and go from there.

Also, can you apply the Click Frenzy "mega sale" concept to your niche? Are there a list of businesses you could contact to conduct a mega sale?

3

USING PSYCHOLOGICAL MARKETING TO CREATE SCARCITY WITHOUT BEING SLIMY

"The only thing more motivating than a limited supply of something is a rapidly diminishing supply of that same thing."
— **Scott Fenstermaker**

Jedi Psychological Marketing Tactics To Create Scarcity And A Frenzy Of Buyers For Your Product

Your favourite performing artist is coming to town. Tomorrow morning at 10 a.m. the tickets go on sale. You are ready at your computer from 9 a.m. You go to the ticketing website and are frantically pressing refresh for one hour. At 10:01 a.m., you press refresh, but the server is crashing because of all the load. And then at 10:03 a.m., you realize that all the tickets are sold.

What is going on here? How do 100,000 tickets get sold in three minutes? How can these events make you so desperate to buy the tickets that you'll waste an hour of your time (some people even line-up overnight in the freezing cold to get tickets), and when you run your poor little business event, you push and push and push for weeks and months and it's a struggle to sell *any* tickets?

To understand the answer to these questions, first we need to open up the history books to see where this all started. Then we need to understand human psychology and why we do these irrational things. Then we need to understand the tactics that these promoters use to sell out these events. And then finally, you can apply these tactics in your scarcity marketing campaigns.

Why Is Scarcity Good?

If there's something you really want, and you think it's in rapidly diminishing supply, you'll do anything to get it RIGHT NOW! It's what psychologist Daniel Kahneman calls "loss aversion." His theories are quite complex, but the root of them is that people are far more strongly motivated to act to avoid a loss than to gain something. Someone who misses out on an exclusive ticket loses more satisfaction than someone who gains satisfaction from a $100 windfall.

A note of caution: This scarcity stuff is really powerful, and it's extremely important that you use it for noble and worthwhile causes. Nothing stinks more than a fake scarcity campaign where people say something like "There's only ten available" when there's really an unlimited quantity available. People know when you're faking it, so don't do it!

A Closely Guarded Scarcity Marketing Tactic From The 1600s That Still Works Today

The earliest example of scarcity marketing is the sixteenth century "tulip bubble" that occurred in Holland. When tulips were first introduced to the Dutch from Turkey in 1593, they were a novelty that quickly became popular and, therefore, somewhat expensive. Then the tulips contracted a non-fatal virus, "mosaic," that didn't kill but altered them so that they had streaks of different colors appearing on their petals, creating a variety of patterns that made them more rare. With tulip bulbs already selling at a premium, those altered by the virus became even more desirable.

Soon everyone wanted to invest and speculate in tulip bulbs, and prices were believed to have no limit. The true bulb buyers began to pre-sell their inventories for the growing season, thus increasing demand for the bulbs as they became more scarce. Prices quickly rose so high that people started trading everything they owned to purchase more tulip bulbs in the belief that they could resell them and make a fortune. Within a month, the overpriced tulip bulbs skyrocketed to twenty times their original value!

But as happens with many speculative bubbles, a few people decided to sell rather than wait for prices to go even higher, and the selling created a domino effect. Soon everyone wanted to sell and few were buying; the lack of buyers caused the prices to drop dramatically, quickly causing people to panic and sell the bulbs for whatever prices they could get. This panic led to dealers refusing to honor contracts. People lost their homes, property, and everything they had of value over a simple flower. A person would have traded an entire estate for a bulb in the beginning, but by the end, a tulip bulb was worth no more than an onion.

The concept of scarcity is so powerful it can change an entire nation's economy!

In 1982, Amram Knishinsky wrote a research study on the purchase decisions of wholesale beef buyers. He observed that they more than doubled their orders when they were told that, because of certain weather conditions overseas, there was likely to be a scarcity of foreign beef in the near future.

But their orders increased 600 percent when they were informed that no one else had that information yet. Scarcity works.

Even Disney has been applying scarcity as a mainstream marketing tactic since 1937. The "Disney vault" idea started when *Snow White and the Seven Dwarfs* was rereleased to the cinemas a few years after it was originally released. Consumers were encouraged to watch the film again in theaters before it was confined again to the "Disney Vault" for an unknown period of time.

Disney uses this vault concept to control its market and to allow Disney films to be fresh for new generations of young children. A side effect of the moratorium process is that videos and DVDs of Disney films placed on moratorium become collectibles, being sold in stores and at auction websites such as eBay for an expensive premium.

Action exercise: Can you see any similarities from these historical examples of scarcity and your current business? How can you apply this scarcity concept today?

The Psychology Of Scarcity

Marilyne and Wyatt Woodsmall are expert behavioral modelers and world class trainers/consultants. This husband and wife team are really smart and their depth of knowledge spans many subjects. They were the Mind Coaches® for the U.S. Olympic diving team. They have modeled, trained, and coached some of the world's leading minds and experts in a variety of fields. While I was writing this book, I mentioned that I was writing a chapter on scarcity and asked them about their thoughts on the subject. They shared my belief that using the scarcity concept should be done with complete integrity. Here are their thoughts:

The Concept Of Scarcity: A Brief Overview

by Marilyne Woodsmall and Wyatt Woodsmall

We would like to clarify a few things about the concept of scarcity, which has found its place in the world of Internet marketing, and in particular, in the context of product launches. The concept of scarcity is not new. Robert Cialdini discussed it in his book *Influence: Science and Practice* in 1984.

He and his graduate students discovered that compliance professionals know that people blindly and mechanically respond to certain things. Furthermore, compliance professionals also know how to trigger these automatic responses.

It all comes down to patterns. In our own work as behavioral modelers and human typologists (the study of human difference) we know that patterns of all types are the basis of the majority of human behaviors. And in our work to enhance human performance, an understanding of these powerful patterns is a critical piece of the puzzle. Such is the case in modeling the best marketing launches as well.

The concept of scarcity itself is indeed a valid one. It is based on the fact that human beings follow set patterns in their behavior. Just like the People Patterns™ that we teach, the scarcity pattern is also outside the realm of one's conscious awareness. And this is one of the reasons why it works with so many unknowing individuals.

Scarcity is a compliance technique that feeds off this unconscious mechanical pattern present in humans and in other species for that matter. It is important to realize that these fixed action patterns make us vulnerable to anyone who knows how they work. We are literally at the mercy of those who know what buttons to push.

Even before the arrival of Internet marketing, we discovered in modeling top salespeople, that they had found out about the concept of scarcity and immediately began using it as one of their weapons. They realized the following basic rule: People are most easily influenced when they believe the source to be scarce or valuable.

The tactics that are used are Limited numbers and Deadlines. In using these tactics, the goal is to make prospects think that they can't have it later, so they want it now. Scarcity plays on the fear of never being able to have the product or service if it is not purchased immediately. From a psychological perspective, we often use availability as a guide to qualify validity. Also, psychologically speaking, when our ability to have something is limited, then we tend to rationalize that the item or product is worth more or has extra qualities.

And in recent years, many Internet marketers have discovered this powerful scarcity tool. They are using it in their product launches in a manner that is not exactly kosher.

You see, there are two ways in which to use this powerful information. Cialdini distinguishes between so called "influence sleuths" and "influence thieves." Unfortunately, most of the people on the Internet who are using scarcity to sell their products fall into the latter category.

Robert Coorey is part of the former, the "influence sleuths." Like all positive marketing experts who care about serving the customer, he understands the fine line between influence and exploitation. Furthermore, he realizes that coming from a place of authenticity will, in the long run, bring loyal customers. Scarcity, thus, can be used effectively with integrity, especially when your bottom line is in a genuine way to help the customer rather than make a quick buck.

In your marketing launches, you want to build genuine excitement around your product. This is where using scarcity effectively will help you to do so, without creating hype and without misleading your customers down a path of later remorse.

In marketing launches, we are moving into a new approach to getting customers. It really is possible to use scarcity with integrity. In this way, you meet the needs of the customers first. Influencing them in a way that creates a win/win not a win/lose is the only way to go.

Reverse-Engineering Apple's Scarcity Marketing Tactics

How come when Apple releases a new phone, there are people sleeping outside the stores for days before the product is released? How come on day one of the iPhone 5 launch, Apple sold 2,000,000 iPhones in twenty-four hours? How does its new phone launch get on the front page of every major newspaper around the world when poor old Nokia can't sell a phone to save itself?

And here's the funny thing: the user interface is basically the same thing since the first iPhone came out in 2007. Each device is thinner or lighter and only adds limited extra functionality. But we're still hungry to buy it.

Apple's secret is that it keeps its secrets, or at least it acts like what it is doing is a big secret until its product is launched, which leads to a lot of speculation among users and the media. Apple is the master at teasing customers with its marketing campaigns, keeping them in suspense until its new product is launched. Apple fuels the buzz by refusing to provide any information for weeks or even months before the release of every iPhone. For example, when Apple announced it would hold a press conference on September 12, 2012, it wouldn't say what the press announcement would be about. This silence caused the media to speculate whether it would be about the new iPhone 5 or something else. All this speculation in the media led to a boost in consumer interest—and for free—Apple didn't even need to advertise to get the buzz started. Only after weeks of this free publicity did Apple spend money on a media campaign to keep the momentum high.

Apple then used the concept of scarcity to further the demand for the new iPhone. Just an hour after the iPhone 5 went on sale for pre-orders on September 14, 2012, the Apple website stated that heavy demand for the product would only allow for preorders of the phone because enough phones were not currently available. The result of this tactic: a record for first-day sales for the iPhone 5, and the phone remained on back order for the next several weeks, thus prolonging the ability (and desirability) of owning one.

At E-Web Marketing, we've adapted Apple's tactics for our book launch clients. When a client is ready to launch a new book, we often just send the book cover as an email to the list, without saying what the book contains, what is the price, or how to order it. As long as the list is engaged, we'll always get a massive response. One time, our poor administration manager got swamped with people wanting to pre-order the book and had to spend all day telling people to be patient!

Reverse-Engineering The Major Event Ticket Marketing Strategy

Remember at the start of this chapter we were talking about how events get sold out in just minutes?

Dean Budnick and Josh Baron were so sick of missing out on major event tickets that they decided to interview 100 people in the events industry, find out all their secrets, and then write a book about it, titled *Ticket Masters*.

Here's the main secret: A very small percentage of seats are available to purchase during the initial general sale.

"Before that time a lot of artists have committed their ticket inventory to credit card companies they have alliances with, to their fan clubs for pre-sale, to the promoter who has a variety of opportunities, to sponsors and to the venue," explains Budnick in the book. "Plus they also keep some inventory for themselves and the secondary market (eBay, Gumtree and other ticket selling websites)."

At Justin Bieber's Nashville show in January 2013, only 7 percent of tickets to the show were available to purchase at the general sale, meaning 93 percent of tickets had already been set aside for other partners.

At Taylor Swift's U.S. concerts, just 15 percent of tickets were available at the advertised on-sale date. For Miley Cyrus' Hannah Montana tour, the numbers were similar, about 15 to 20 percent.

Action exercise: What does this mean for you as a marketer trying to sell out an event? Can you release a limited number of tickets for general sale, and then sell tickets through other channels? What other businesses or channels would be a good candidate to sell your tickets? Write down five ideas below:

1. _____

2. _____

3. _____

4. _____

5. _____

How CatchOfTheDay Sells An Item Every Second, 24/7

CatchOfTheDay is Australia's number one shopping website. Here's some stats about the business it does:

- CatchOfTheDay started in October 2006 with five employees and a small warehouse. Since then the team has expanded to 600 full-time staff working from two huge distribution centres.

- On average, one item is sold every 1 second, 24 hours a day, 7 days a week.

- Web traffic data agency Hitwise named CatchOfTheDay.com. au Australia's number one shopping site with 14.73 percent of all retail traffic from Australia. The only retail website with higher traffic was U.S. giant Amazon.com.

- CatchOfTheDay is currently host to over 2 million registered members. The membership base has grown through word-of-mouth alone, which is testament to the value we offer.

- In a period of 24 hours, it sold 4,300 Toshiba laptops, 320,000 Ferrero Rocher chocolates, and more than $1.4m worth of Samsung TVs.

Lucky for you, I've done some analysis on CatchOfTheDay and I've reverse-engineered some of its closely guarded secrets for success!

Product Title
Product tag-line   03:47:44

In the above image, two pieces of scarcity advertising are being used. The banner "HURRY – ALMOST GONE!" makes you urgently want to click on the image, and the timer on the bottom right telling you how much longer the offer will last makes you want to hurry up as well! Let's investigate this a bit further.

When you click-through to the product listing page, here's what you see:

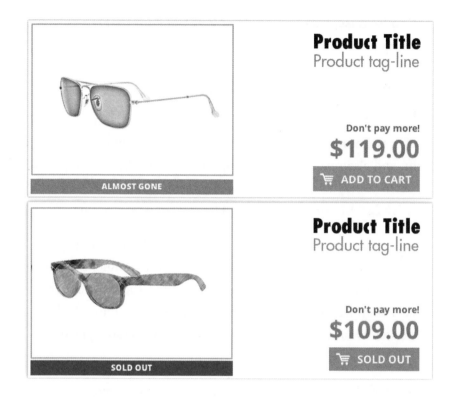

So one of the glasses is almost gone, and one is sold out. Real proof that the range is almost gone. If you want the gold/green glasses, you better hurry up!

After you add the gold/green glasses to your cart, there is a message near the header that says: "Stock is not reserved until you complete checkout." This is brilliant marketing. The company is forcing you to check out quickly and not abandon your cart so you don't lose the stock. Also, the site makes a limit of five per customer—see the research from Brian Wansink below to learn more about why this works so well!

CatchOfTheDay also uses these scarcity tactics with its Facebook marketing. One of its recent Facebook posts said:

> "Woah, we've sold almost 2,000 pairs of Ugg boots in 2 hours.
> These will sell out guys, don't miss out!"

Action exercise: Can you apply any of CatchOfTheDay's scarcity techniques to your offering?

Secret Pricing Formulas To Maximize Sales And Profits

Pricing is a funny thing. It's one of the most challenging areas to get right, and also one of the most important. Brian Wansink did some excellent scientific research on pricing in his book *Mindless Eating: Why We Eat More Than We Think*. Here's what he has to say:

> A while back, I teamed up with two professor friends of mine— Steve Hoch and Bob Kent—to see if anchoring influences how much food we buy in grocery stores. We believed that grocery shoppers who saw numerical signs such as "Limit 12 Per Person" would buy much more than those who saw signs such as "No Limit Per Person."

> To nail down the psychology behind this, we repeated this study in different forms, using different numbers, different promotions (like "2 for $2"), and in different supermarkets and convenience stores. By the time we finished, we knew that almost any sign with a number promotion leads us to buy 30 to 100 percent more than we normally would.

I've personally been sucked in by this advertising. My local supermarket has a limit on the baby formula that you can buy. Limit 4 per person. The first time I saw this, it made me feel like the formula was in scarce supply so I ended up buying all four tins of formula! Then the next time I went to buy it, the same sign was there, so I didn't get sucked in by the scarcity marketing tactics! I showed them!

Eben Pagan has sold over $100 million in info products. He knows what he's doing. Remember how for his most recent Accelerate launch he had a 50 percent early bird discount for the first five days only, and after that, the price doubled back to the regular full price? This strategy encourages fast action.

Pure profit upsells can work magic with information products. To maximise sales for E-Web Marketing's information marketing clients, we normally have a "one-time offer" at the time of purchase. It's common for over 25 percent of people to take these "one-time offers." In the free book resources page (http://www.feedastarvingcrowd. com/resources), you can download the HTML template and wording we use for our "one-time offer pages"—it will blow your mind!

Keep Raising Your Prices

At E-Web, between 2004 and 2011, each year we continually raised our setup prices, and for five years running, our business won the award for the Deloitte Fast 50, honoring the fifty fastest-growing companies in the Asia Pacific region. Recently, our business model changed so we don't have setup fees anymore, but you can see how consistently raising our pricing (and the value our clients received for this pricing) actually helped grow our business.

Starter packages— setup fees	Economy	Business	Executive	Silver	Gold	Platinum
2004	$495	$1,495	$2,495			
2006	$695	$1,495	$2,495			
2007	$895	$1,495	$2,495			
2008	$1,995	$3,995	$5,995			
2009	$2,490	$4,990	$7,490			
2009	$2,490	$4,990	$7,490	$9,990	$14,990	$19,990
2011	$4,990	$7,490	$9,990	$14,990	$19,990	$24,990

Action exercise: Are your prices too low? Is there any opportunity for you to raise your prices? Can you apply any of the pricing tactics above to your business?

An Inexpensive Wordpress Plugin That Achieved A Sales Page Buy Boost By 80% In A Recent Split Test

There's a cool WordPress plug-in called Scarcity Samurai. I've met the development team members behind this plug-in, and they are a switched-on bunch of lads. They shared with me the case study of how they applied scarcity at four different points in the sales cycle and how it boosted conversion overall by 453 percent.

- The first thing they did was get a landing page boost of 40 percent from adding the banner timer.

- Then, Scarcity Samurai achieved an email open rate boost of 20 percent, just by adding the words "ends tomorrow" to the subject line.

- They achieved an email click-through rate boost (20 percent) from adding the exact amount of time left that the deal was valid.

- And they achieved a sales page buy boost of 80 percent from adding a banner timer similar to the landing page.

The overall campaign boost (no scarcity vs. mega scarcity) was 453 percent. It's a great idea to add as many of these elements as possible to your next campaign. All of the screenshots from the campaign are in the free book resources section (http://www.feedastarvingcrowd. com/resources).

Action Exercise: Can you add any of the scarcity elements above to your campaign?

What Converts Better, Story Or Data?

I'm a logical person. I get persuaded by facts and figures. But turns out I'm in the minority. A Carnegie Mellon University study comprehensively tested the effectiveness of using either a story or data to persuade people to donate to an African charity. The data pitch spoke about food shortages, lack of rain, and millions of homeless people. The story pitch spoke about Rokia, an African girl who was starving. The test subjects were shown her photo and asked to donate to help her directly.

On average, the data subjects donated $1.14 each. And the story subjects donated $2.38 each, more than double the amount.

Even more interesting, the researchers thought they would get smart and try to combine facts with the story of Rokia. But the third test, the facts plus story, only got $1.43 per person.

"If I look at the mass, I will never act," said Mother Teresa. "If I look at the one, I will."

If you want people to act, the data says to tell them a story!

Scientific Research That Shows How Many Product Choices You Should Offer

More choice is better, right? Give people more options and they are more likely to buy. While this sounds good in theory, it actually doesn't work too well when you try it out in real life.

A Columbia university study found that too much choice is actually de-motivating for consumers, and when there are too many choices, they actually make NO choice. As the old saying goes "a confused mind does nothing."

Researchers set up a jam-tasting stall in a posh supermarket in California. Sometimes, they offered six varieties of jam, at other times twenty-four. Jam tasters were then offered a voucher to buy jam at a discount.

While more choice attracted more customers to look, very few of them actually bought jam. The display that offered less choice made many more sales—in fact, only 3 percent of jam tasters at the twenty-four-flavour stand used their discount vouchers, versus 30 percent at the six-flavour stand.

My friend Dale Beaumont runs a multi-million dollar business training company, and he only has two products for sale—an $8,000 membership and a $13,000 membership. He used to run five different businesses, and he had many different price points in each business. Since simplifying to this new model, his sales have increased and his business is far simpler to manage. Dale has also simplified his schedule. He now works two months in the business, then takes a month off, then works two months in the business, and then takes a month off. What a great lifestyle!

The problem when you give people too much choice is that they try to "maximize" the decision. A "maximiser," as Barry Schwartz mentions in *The Paradox of Choice*, is someone who will exhaustively search all the options, seeking all possible information, in order to make the best possible choice. This behavior generally consumes a lot of time, and it often leads to nagging doubts. Barry Schwartz's work on the paradox of choice even found that maximisers are prime candidates for depression.

So you're doing people's health a service by offering less choice, and when you offer less choice, your bottom line should be healthier as well.

Action Exercise: Look at your product offerings. Is there too much choice there? How can you simplify this further?

4

WRITING COPY SO PEOPLE PULL OUT THEIR WALLETS AND BUY

"Advertising is salesmanship mass produced. No one would bother to use advertising if he could talk to all his prospects face-to-face. But he can't."
— **Morris Hite**

Many people underestimate how much copy you actually need to convince people to take an action. Most prospective customers don't wake up in the morning and want to buy your product for no reason at all. They generally need a lot of persuasion.

Here's some examples of how much copy we did for a recent webinar launch:

- Five-part email sequence to encourage registrations (1,000 words)

- Five-part "stick" reminder email sequence to improve attendance rate (1,200 words)

- Thank you email for registering (183 words)

- Thank you email for buying (300 words)

- Three-part upsell email sequence (728 words)

- Five-part post-webinar email sequence for attendees who were non-buyers (1,500 words)

- Fifty-seven webinar slides (2,200 words)

- Webinar registration page (300 words)

- Webinar thank you page (200 words)

- Sales/order page (780 words)

- One time offer upsell page (1,080 words)

- Order thank you page (200 words)

Total words for this campaign were approximately 10,000 words—almost a small novel!

At the free book resources page (http://www.feedastarvingcrowd.com/resources), there's a link so you can download the sequence and flow chart of the campaign. There was a lot of complexity, and it's easier to understand when you can see it all zoomed up.

Here's some examples of how much copy we wrote for a recent national speaking tour campaign:

- Video script for registration page (500 words)

- Cover letter to send out tickets in the mail (283 words)

- Landing page for free opt-in (301 words)

- Registration page (2,104 words)

- Seventeen follow-up emails to get registrations (3,400 words)

- Five "stick" emails to ensure people actually attend the event (1,304 words)

Total: Over 7,900 words

You need a lot of copy to drive people to take an action.

Two Lessons I Learnt From The World's Top Copywriter

About ten years ago, I learnt two very valuable lessons from Gary Halbert. I've used these lessons very successfully ever since. These lessons are so obvious, but so brilliant at the same time.

Lesson #1: Your readers are bored.

Lesson #2: Everyone reads your copy by himself at his computer.

You can apply these two lessons in tandem. Most people are bored at work, bored at home, bored when they go out. It's all just too boring. When they are browsing around on the web and they come across your brilliant content, you are actually doing them a favour by providing something that is interesting.

And everyone is alone when he or she is reading your sales copy. You're not talking to an audience of 1,000 people. You're having a personal conversation with one person. What does this mean? It means you can get emotional, and it means you should write your copy with the frame of mind you would have in writing a personal letter to a friend.

Templates And "Fill-In-The-Blank" Headlines Plus Strategies For Writing Good Headlines

While I was writing this book, I interviewed Alexi Neocleous, one of Australia's top copywriters. Alexi is the man behind a lot of high-profile campaigns, and he's on the speed dial of many top online marketers.

The first thing I asked him was "If I strip away every single headline and little tip and trick you've got and only leave you with one head-line to use, what would that be?"

Without taking a breath, he said it would be the "How to" headline. The reason why is that it's the most universally applicable and diverse headline there is—because it promises to offer a solution. It promises to solve a problem; it promises to give information.

Alexi recommends to use the headline "how to—*insert benefit*"

How to lose five pounds. How to grow ripe red tomatoes. How to get at the top of Google. Or it could be how to solve a pain. How never again to slice a golf ball. Or how to cure frustrating slicing. How to put an end to your kids' ADD.

So that's the absolute basic one. Then as markets evolve, and people have seen your claims before, you need to start adding specifics—for example, specific claims, specific proof, etc.

As an example, "How to lose five kilos" is really a claim that's been said many times. But you can do: How to lose five kilos by eating more butter. How to lose five kilos by eating twice as much bread as you are now. How to lose five kilos without ever exercising for more than a minute per day.

These little specifics add surprise to the main benefits and lead people to ask themselves, "Wow, what's that about? I haven't seen that before."

The key to a great headline is surprise.

If someone is surprised, he will want to read more. And then you've done your job.

What Makes A Great Sub-Headline?

It's a good idea to accompany your great headline with a subhead. For example, Alexi is running a great campaign in the real estate market. Here's the headline and subhead:

How To Uncover The Hottest Growth In Cash Flow Areas Before Other Investors

Two magic indicators used by a street smart property investor who bought fifteen properties before his twenty-seventh birthday

This headline works well for several reasons. Property investors are always wanting to know how to get capital growth or cash flow. They're really wanting to know how to find cash flow, and they're always wondering how can they get a leg up on other investors. So that's why there's the headline, "How to uncover the hottest growth in cash flow areas before other investors."

But that's not necessarily a new claim, which is why in the subhead there is specificity: *fifteen properties before his twenty-seventh birthday.* Now you take it all as a collaborative; you've got yourself a headline and subhead that's really never gone to market before.

After reading this great headline and subhead, I wanted to find out exactly what was Alexi's method for writing headlines. Here's what he said:

> What I want to get across here, it's easy to get caught up in strategies and tactics. The key to writing really great headlines is understanding the market. You can know all the strategies and all the tactics. But if you really don't understand where your market's at, what their worries and their fears and their desires, really what their path is that they've already walked down; you will never ever write really good headlines.
>
> Understanding the market is never a quick and easy process. It does take time to learn and do some of the things that I do to understand the market; I read the magazines they read. I visit the websites they visit. I read the emails they read, and that means subscribing to the same e-zines that they subscribe to.

I go to the same discussion boards. I buy the same products. And really I do what they do. The situations where I've written the best headlines is where I fall into the market myself, which means I really understand it.

But if I were to give you some magical stuff here, let me give you a list of words that will help to improve just the news worthiness and the surprise of your headlines. So here are some words that I keep revisiting time and time again. Words like:

- Secrets

- Quick

- Easy

- Instantly

- Anything with the word "you" in it

- How to

- Fast

- At last

- Discovery

- Amazing

These are newsworthy sorts of terms. People just really do love to be fascinated. They're looking for a certain spark in their day. This is why it's always a good idea, if you're really keen on learning how to get people's attention, to read tabloid magazine covers: *National Enquirer* and stuff. It's all cheap, dirty stuff that they talk about, but I tell you those teasers are just incredible. "Confessions of" whoever, and this is what rings true to people's psyche more than anything else.

Spend time studying those, using words that I've just spoken about them. What else you can do is really understand, and we'll talk about this more in a bit; really understand what drives human nature. Like the seven deadly sins. If you look at human history over hundreds, and even thousands of years, you're going to see the seven deadly sins pop up time and time again, in gluttony, lust, and other ways. That usually is what drives human nature. Maslow's hierarchy of needs—again, there's a lot of good stuff that's applicable to human nature.

If you just spend some time thinking about your market, really: How do they operate in accordance to the seven deadly sins? Where does envy kick in? Where does gluttony kick in? Where does greed kick in? You can see, time and time again, they rise.

That's the most important psychology of a market. Like right now, for the property company, we're doing some joint ventures with some people who buy and sell websites, and these people have found a nice little niche in the market because they've found that when they target property investor lists, property investors are loving it. Why? Because they're able to draw on parallels between renovating a house and flipping a house, and flipping a website.

So this is first in market stuff now, so they're able to say some very basic stuff. Now when you buy and flip a home, you've got to deal with the bank. You've got to put up a lot of money. You've got to deal with tradespeople. Often it takes many, many months to get your money back. There's risk; there's all sorts of things. Lawyers have to get involved, etcetera. But you know what? You can buy and flip a website much more easily, and sometimes make much more cash flow with less risk.

And now they've got these little parallels that kick in; they're almost first in market. So just drawing those parallels is brand new, and property investors are going crazy for it.

Action Exercise: Go to the top online news sites or blogs in your niche and make a list of the article headlines that have the most shares, likes, and comments. This is the best way to see what content your market is most engaged with.

Anatomy Of A Winning Sales Page

Again, I asked Alexi to share his expertise on what makes a winning sales page, and here's his response.

> Let's do the anatomy of a winning sales letter. You've got different formulas that you can use, and you've got the AIDA formula: Attention, Interest, Desire, and Action. You've got much more evolved ones than that, which I'm about to share now. When you're talking a sales letter you're needing multiple pages, so if it's one to two pages you could probably just get away with the AIDA formula.
>
> But if you're looking at 8, 10, 12, 14, 16, or 18 pages and beyond, or if you're looking at twelve-plus minutes in a video sales letter, you need something much more diverse. And that's because you're often speaking to a market that needs more meat. You're often speaking to a market where they need more information to make the decision. That's either because they're more evolved or because what you're selling is at a price point where they just need more convincing.
>
> An AIDA formula takes one or two pages and you're asking for like a free trial for something for $20. Maybe that does the job. Or the AIDA formula over one or two pages that you're sending to your customer list of people who have bought it time and time again; they trust you, they don't need as much. But if you're talking an evolved audience for a product that's maybe $100 or more, you need more.

Building Attention and Interest

So here's the one that I use. You start off with attention, and this is where you usually are focusing on great headlines, and really assessing where the market is at. What sort of a headline here is going to get their attention? Once you get their attention you need to build up their interests. Depending on the product, you could tell a story, you could hit on some problem hot buttons. You could ask them the questions. But you really have seconds now to build up their interest.

Once you've got their interest, you've bought a bit more time, maybe 10, 15, 20 seconds. This is where you need to start to convey your proof. Now for me, I'm giving you a very linear left brain process. For me, attention and credibility is built in together at once. So if I make a claim, usually my next sentence is the proof. "Did you know that amongst medical professions, vets have the highest rate of suicide, the highest rate of depression, and the highest rate of alcoholism? It's true. A study done by the Vet Board in the U.S. found that."

That's a situation where I've asked a question to get their interest, and then I move straight into credibility to prove what I'm saying, as opposed to spending half a page building interest. And then I'll say, "Hi, my name is...etcetera." So usually that's what I do—just get that proof much earlier. But for the sake of this formula, we have attention, we have interest, and we have credibility, and then we have proof yet again—a different type of proof. If credibility before was a testimonial, this time it could be demonstration. If before it was demonstration, this time it could be testimonial. I'm having two shots here at credibility and proof, but they are two sides of the same coin.

Painting A Picture Of The Future

Then we start to move into benefits. We'll either paint word pictures, or we may future pace and describe what their life could be like if they potentially buy the product. If it's an information product, we customarily move into bullet points here. We have great bullet points that just really zing where every single bullet point is like "Wow, what's that?" and "Wow, what's this?" and "Wow, that's incredible; I've never heard of that before." Just to get them really excited.

At this point, we'll definitely introduce a unique selling point (USP)—"Other products on weight loss they'll tell you to do this and they'll tell you to do this. Mine doesn't do any of that. In fact, mine is the easiest thing you'll ever find. In fact, mine is the only one that promises to do this, and it's written by a doctor. Or it's written by a person who has lost over 102 kilos."

Bringing Home The Sale

Once we've spent quite a bit of time talking about the benefits and articulating the USP, we'll usually move on to scarcity now. We start to move into our offer here. We start to move into details of why you should buy. "Normally, if you were to sit down with me, it would be $1,000.00 an hour. So if you come to a gig where I'm speaking three days straight, eight hours a day, it would be $24,000.00. You don't have to pay $24,000.00 because I'll get you in a room. You don't have to pay $15,000.00. You don't have to pay $10,000.00—you can pay only $997.00."

Now we start to get scarcity kicking in. We start to get the offer kicking in, and we start to take away the sale here. "There's only fifty tickets available at this price and this message is going out to 97,450 people on my email list. I plan for this to sell out any time soon." So this is where we move on to action. Explicit order instructions.

Time To Add A Warning

And once you have very clear instructions, you move on to warning. You start to do the pain and the promise. Just a word of warning; you might say, "You may be thinking, 'Is the money worth it, should I attend?' And I ask you to consider what would your life be like in three months' time, in six months' time, in nine months' time, and in twelve months' time, if you don't take action."

And then we move into the pleasure side of it. Just imagine you fast forward a year down the track. You've taken this small chance, this little baby step. You've dipped your toe in the water, and then in one year's time, what can your life look like if this, if that, and so forth. So again, we're using word pictures to give them an alternate reality.

And then we move into specific greed-based "act now" type things. Usually, we'll have a situation where if you register now, or in the next ten days, I'm also going to chuck in a bonus or two. So it's really get them to act now; give them a logical reason to act now.

Wrapping It All Up

I've made the formula sound quite linear, but the truth is proof is usually mixed all the way throughout. The truth is spoken and unspoken benefits and is peppered all throughout the letter. When we get to the close, scarcity is sort of sprinkled throughout the close in every point. And in some ways, scarcity is sprinkled even in the open, when we start to talk about it, for example, it could be "This is the first time that I've ever shared this content before. Normally, you'd have to get access to me via one-on-one consulting."

Even though I've given you a linear formula, for really great copy, at any moment you could miss out on this—that's just unspoken and spoken all the way throughout. It's very subtle. Great copy—you don't see the selling. Great copy—you don't see the nuance. You don't feel like you're being sold; you're so hooked into the message that you don't notice that you're ordering until you're ordering. You don't see how the sausage is made; you don't see the mechanics. If at any time you notice mechanics, it's probably not great copy.

In the free book resources section (http://www.feedastarvingcrowd.com/resources), I have some links for you to view world class sales page copy. Enjoy!

Advanced Copywriting Techniques

I then drilled Alexi down to find out his most advanced copywriting techniques. Stuff that not many people know about, like future pacing, and including emotional elements in the story. The good stuff. Here it is:

Let's talk about emotion. The most important and best way to get emotion into a copy is to tell stories. That bypasses almost all the filters. That bypasses all the lacking belief that we can have when we say, "You're going to feel like this," "You're going to feel like that," and "You're going to be doing this." No, tell stories. That's just the safest way, the least chance of screwing it up.

With future pacing, it's interesting. I do use future pacing, only after I've comprehensively claimed and proven that I know what I'm talking about. Future pacing is really hard to do if they don't believe you. So use that one with care. Future pacing is describing in detail the emotions and the life situations and the benefits at a future time of what your prospects are going to experience.

Now, often it's not needed if you've got a great story. Like if you, for example, lost a whole bunch of weight, telling your story in vivid detail is in a form future pacing for your readers because they start to superimpose their own lives into the story. There are things in our brain called mirror neurons that activate when we hear a great story that we empathise with.

And usually, I'll future pace after I've done all the benefits, I've laid the groundwork for the proof. They want the product; they believe me. Then I might have a "five ways you'll benefit" type thing.

Here's an example of how Alexi has used future pacing in some sales copy:

Your Life-Long Struggle With Food And Your Figure Could Finally Be Over

The small changes to your daily routine in this book could help you lose excess pounds permanently—without willpower, dieting, or spending long hours in the gym every day. Once you follow these simple steps, you could finally:

- Stop nasty food cravings

- Drop a dress size or two

- End overeating

- Overcome an embarrassing bloated stomach

- Shrink wobbly problem areas

- And have more energy, be stronger, look better, and feel more attractive than you have in years

My next question for Alexi was: How do you write in a way that is informal, conversational, and easy-to-read?

> So a quick and easy thing that I use is the Flesch-Kincaid scale. (You can see this by checking Grammar in Microsoft Word.)
>
> I use that every day. Because I write so often, what I'm looking for is passive sentences of 5 percent or less, and a reading grade score of Year 7 or Year 8. It's very rare I get into 9s and 10s, and if I do, it's often because of medical stuff in emails. Sometimes, it's just unavoidable and I try to get my best to get it down to Year 7, Year 8. Sometimes, it's impossible, but I don't kill myself when that happens. It happens like two or three times out a hundred.
>
> If I have more than one idea in a sentence, that's where the problems start to arise. So you really want one idea per sentence. And the way to avoid more than one idea is to use a full stop. All in all, the Flesch-Kincaid scale will tell you, though. As soon as you start to hit Year 9 and 10, often that's because your sentence is too long, or you're using long words. So the first thing to do is use a full stop. Pull that sucker out and start to substitute long words for short words.

And Alexi's number one ultimate form of proof is what he calls "the dramatic demonstration." For any products you're selling, digital or physical, the strongest and most powerful content should be front and centre of the pitch.

Here are a few examples of "dramatic demonstrations" from the offline world:

> **Godfrey's Vacuums:** They had the Godfrey's bowling bowl test. So their claim was the strongest sucking power of any vacuum on the market today. But that's in abstract terms, like really, is it believable? And what does it really mean? And so on the

commercial you will see the vacuum suck up a twelve-pound bowling ball or whatever. That's just incredible proof.

Otis Elevators: Way back in the early twentieth century, Otis wanted to prove that his safety brake could save lives, so if an elevator cable were to snap, people wouldn't die. And so he perched himself up many levels in the elevator. He would actually put himself on a little container, and then cut the line, and his safety break would kick in and save his own life. He would do that in front of hundreds and thousands of people live. Within a year or two, Otis Elevators was born and became very successful, even after years of struggling.

Action exercise: Are there any demonstrations you can use in your marketing communication?

Anatomy Of A Winning Video Sales Letter

Alexi is a huge fan of video sales letters (VSL). And with good reason. They sell like crazy! But you need to get the formula right. It's quite easy for these to go very, very wrong if you have any of the puzzle pieces missing.

This is an advanced strategy, so only use it if you already have a sales page that is converting. Let me show you what a world-class video sales letter looks like. Go to www.capturehim.com for a great VSL example.

You'll notice a couple of things on this VSL page:

1. There's no header navigation.

2. There's no text on the page trying to sell you anything until the sales pitch is ready.

3. The "magic buy button" comes up underneath the video only once the sales pitch is ready (about 10 minutes in).

4. There's no video player controls. You can't scroll forward or backward or see how long there is to go. You can just play or pause. That's all.

5. If you try to leave the page, you get a pop up asking whether you really want to leave and to sign up for the free report.

In Chapter 9, I will cover video sales letters in a lot more detail. But I wanted to give you Alexi's opinion on them to whet your appetite. So how do you make one of these bad boys for yourself? From Alexi:

> You can adapt the sales letter formula that I used before to video sales letters. There are a few caveats, though, and one of those is the first ninety seconds. With normal sales letters, people can scan and scroll and whatever. Still, the opening remains critically important, but nowhere near as important as with the video sales letter.
>
> And in the first ninety seconds, you really want something quite shocking and unexpected. A screen shot of proof, a shocking before and after, something controversial, something that just makes them pause and stop. I'll give you an example; we're doing a test for one of my clients. And the video analytic software shows that about eight or nine minutes into the video, there was one slide that caused them to replay and pause and replay in a very big way.
>
> So I looked at that and I thought, "Beautiful! I'm going to grab that slide and stick it within the first ninety seconds, and use it as an open loop." So for example, "Stay tuned because shortly you are going to discover, you're going to learn about a nutrient that's got 500 percent more DHA than fish oil. Yes, 500 percent. I'll give you the full details in a moment."
>
> Now, I know from the analytics that people want to know what that is because when that slide appeared later on, they replayed it and paused, so they were really keen to know what that was.

So that became an open loop, like a cliffhanger, that I imposed in the video sales letter in the first ninety seconds.

Don't get too caught up with graphics. Those words on screen ones are great. Insert some images here and there if you want. They work really well. You can follow the format that I said earlier. Voice over, just have a clear voice. You can go to Fiverr and find people there who can do it cost affordably. And in terms of creating the video sales letter, the absolute easiest way is to use a software called Audacity and just get it audio recorded. It's a free software.

And then get a virtual assistant on oDesk to merge the audios with slides using Camtasia or whatever they use. My point is, it doesn't have to become a big production to make these things a lucrative profit centre for your business.

Depending on what we're selling, video sales letters are always near the top of the list of the highest converting mediums. It's very rare that I see video not increase response. So if you've got words on a page and it's doing okay, expect some sort of an increase with a video. That's a very safe bet. And nowadays, I mean even if you're doing like a talking head video where you're looking down a camera, it's just so easy to do. Don't get too caught up with production; just get the damn thing done.

Magic buy buttons—if you expect to sell off the page, I would definitely integrate a magic buy button, which is relatively easy to do nowadays.

To be clear, a magic buy button is an "order now" button that doesn't appear on the page until you make your pitch. So, where you start to talk about how you get the product, and stuff like that. That's where you want your magic buy to appear. And the reason why you don't show the buy now button from the start is because depending on your traffic source, you don't

want it to tip your hand that you're selling something. That's
the main reason—you want them to think that you're going to
have it in content, and often you really want good information
in your video sales letter anyway. So that's why. I found time
and time again the best time for it is when it's clear and obvious
that you're making your pitch; then the buy button appears.

Why Your Prospect's Biggest Pain Points Are The Ones They Don't Want You To Know, And How To Get To The Bottom Of Them

Alexi really got deep here and revealed some of his most advanced
copywriting tactics:

> When you are thinking about your market, think of it as
> having multiple layers. Think of those layers as having the rea-
> sons people tell strangers for why they buy something. These
> are people they don't trust; this is where you get the worst sort
> of responses in a survey.

> Then you've got the people who could be family or friends,
> people with whom they open up a bit, and then you've got the
> reasons they tell themselves. And the reasons, they don't really
> know what they are. So an example could be a middle aged
> guy who buys a sports car. He'll tell his friends he bought the
> sports car because it goes from nought to 100 in five seconds.
> "I bought the sports car because I love to feel the acceleration."
> These are sort of the open "will tell" sort of benefits. "I bought
> the sports car because I got a great deal; I screwed down the
> salesperson."

> Then we move into "Won't tell." These are usually to do with
> social engineering situations. What others will think of me.
> And the male who is fifty who has just bought a sports car is
> usually thinking about relationships with women. He's usually

thinking of impressing his friends. He's usually thinking this is a status symbol. "I am a successful business person." Usually, that's what he's thinking.

Then you've got the "can't tell" benefits. This is where we start to move into real deep survival mechanisms here. This is usually to do with a man wanting to have sex appeal basically. Being an alpha male. Being a man that's not going to die on his own. You really can't talk about those to a man, though; you really cannot use that in your copy. At best, all you can do is tell a story.

You may have unspoken images. Actually, there's a great example again in Breakthrough Advertising, where they wanted to get more men to smoke and so they fell squarely into these "won't tell, can't tell" benefits. They couldn't say in the ads, "You'll be more virile," "You'll be more appealing to women," or "You'll be stronger." You can't do any of that stuff. They asked themselves a question: What is an image that typifies masculinity in the eyes of most men?

And back then it was the cowboy. The cowboy in the tight jeans and the boots and the rugged looking face, and the cowboy hat, and so forth. "Wow, this is the rugged man. This man typifies what it means to be a virile strong alpha male." And that's how the Marlboro Man was born.

You're looking for imagery often or stories that convey implicit meaning. You know if you wear a Rolex, what does that mean about you? What does that mean compared to a Casio, or whatever it may be? If you drive a Bentley, what does that mean about you compared to driving a Toyota as an example.

Even the initial imagery of the iPod, if you remember the images they had; it was like the silhouette of people dancing and they had their iPods in their hands and the headphones on. They were selling the experience.

Again, these are all "won't tell, can't tell" benefits.

Casinos also play on these "won't tell, can't tell" benefits. You would think people just want to win money at a casino, but that's not the only motivation. When guys imagine themselves gambling, they conjure up images of themselves as the center of attention and acting like James Bond. No casino promotion says explicitly you will be the centre of attention. Instead, the ads show this in pictures.

Action exercise: Write out five "won't tell, can't tell" benefits for your market. How can you use these in your marketing?

1. _____

2. _____

3. _____

4. _____

5. _____

Free Book Resources: One Of The World's Top Public Speakers Reveals His Secrets For Telling An Engaging Story

My friend Sam Cawthorn is one of the world's top public speakers; he speaks in front of 100,000 people every year and can command up to $50,000 for a single speech!

One of the reasons he is in such high demand is that he is a master at building anticipation and storytelling. After seeing him speak a number of times, I decided to pick his brain and find out exactly how he manages to do it. Our interview went for over thirty minutes, so I was unable to reprint the entire interview in this book. Sam breaks down one of his keynote stories and shows step-by-step how he uses anticipation and surprise to keep the audience engaged throughout the speech.

The good news is that I have the interview available for you to download in the free book resources section (http://www.feedastarv-ingcrowd.com/resources).

5

PROVEN AND BATTLE-TESTED WEB DESIGNS THAT CONVERT

"If design isn't profitable, then it's art."
— **Henrik Fiskar**

Copy is more important than design. One of my mentors has a horrible site; it's just a massive long page that tells all about him. It would get last place at a design contest. But I still engaged him to be my mentor because the content on that page was so damn good!

You might be wondering whether design actually matters at all then? Well, yes it does. It's like the icing on the cake. If my mentor had a better laid out site with attractive images, he would attract even more clients. I am a hardened and cynical marketer so the layout of the site doesn't bother me. But my wife would never do business on a site that didn't look professional because she wouldn't be able to trust it.

In this chapter, we're going to look at many real-life examples of landing pages that convert like crazy. Stuff I've done and stuff that others have done. We're also going to look at sales pages that are kicking butt in the real world as well.

Let's say you do your job right and the customer wants to buy something from you, but once he gets to your checkout, it's really easy for things to get screwed up. I'm going to share with you some checkout strategies I've learnt and applied from the best in the business—these will blow your mind. It amazes me how most websites are making really simple mistakes with their checkout process that leads to huge cart abandonment because it's all too hard. You won't have that problem anymore after going through this chapter.

And finally, we're going to look at a few "out-of-the-box" ways to squeeze names and emails. Save the best for last!

Let's get into it.

Anatomy Of Battle-Tested Landing Pages

Ryan Deiss is a well-known online marketer. He is known for testing and testing and testing fanatically until he gets a design that converts predictably.

This is Ryan's top performing landing page of all time:

Why Is This Landing Page So Good?

Simplicity. It gets straight to the point; there are no navigation elements to confuse people. No images that may or may not help conversions. Just a simple promise and instruction to the customer to enter his email address. The red arrow pointing to the email box is a nice touch, and the call to action "Click Here to Continue" leaves nothing to chance. Deiss has really appealed to the lowest common denominator here!

What Are The Problems With This Landing Page?

First, it's not going to win any design awards, and that means that it will be hard for you to get this sort of squeeze page approved by your client or management team. I mean, there's not even one image!

Second, you've got no chance of getting this approved on Google AdWords or many of the ad networks; they hate landing pages like this. They want you to send people to a site that looks like it has content. Google's goal is for its searchers to have a great experience using Google. And going to pages like this is a great experience for me and you, the marketers, but not for the poor old searcher who likes to get free content without having to opt-in first. So to get this page Google-approved, you're going to need header navigation links, footer navigation links, and also more content on the page describing what it's all about.

Here's a better-looking landing page from Deiss:

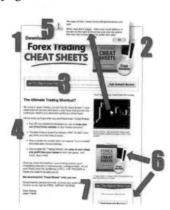

Important Elements:

1. Attention-getting headline

2. Graphic of lead magnet

3. Horizontal opt-in bar

4. Compelling short-form copy

5. Javascript warning popup

6. Compelling captions under each lead magnet component

7. Below-fold opt-in form

This landing page has a much better chance of being approved by your client or management team because there are some styling elements on here, and yes, there are a few pictures too.

Let's go through each element:

1. The headline is strongly written, easy-to-read, with bold black and red text on a white background and looks "professional."

2. Image of what people are actually downloading. It makes sense to show people what they are actually getting!

3. Full-length horizontal opt-in bar. Well, you can't miss it!

4. Deiss is using short copy with only four bullets. His view is that you don't need a whole lot of copy to get people to download a free "lead magnet." I tend to agree, although I've had success with both long and short copy....

5. When you click on the video, a JavaScript warning pops up and tells you that you first need to enter your email to get access to watch the video.

6. The captions underneath each lead magnet describe what they are, and they further encourage you to enter your details in the form.

7. There's a second opt-in form below the fold. This is a good idea to use because you can get the "scrollers" who like to read down the page, and they don't have to come back up again.

The Webinar Opt-In Page That Got 7,991 Registrations With Less Than $2,000 Advertising Spend

I'm extremely proud of this webinar landing page, primarily because the results were so damn good! My team sent a truckload of traffic to this page both from the house email list and also cold traffic from Facebook ads. The design is simple, and the copy is compelling. The copy is based on the top symptoms that most women are feeling when their health is not optimal. Any person who has these symptoms would be compelled to register for the online event.

A few things we also found were really interesting:

1. Almost an equal number of people signed up for the first session at 5 p.m. as the second session at 7 p.m.—it's important to offer two sessions!

2. Show rate was 60 percent—very high for an online seminar. That's because we had five follow-up emails that hyped up the event and a mobile phone text reminder.

3. Time got the better of us and we didn't even get to make the page mobile-responsive, so mobile users had to pinch and zoom to enter their details—and we still had a 40 percent opt-in rate. Now all our landing pages are mobile-responsive designs.

4. We used a link that allows people to "check their local time"— very important because people were logging in from all over the world.

Below is a wireframe of what the page looked like. You can see the copy we used for this page in the free book resources section (http://www.feedastarvingcrowd.com/resources).

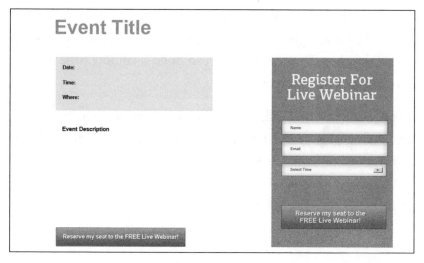

The "Coming Soon" Page That Has Over 7 Million People Registered And Has Been Proven To Work In Over 100 Different Industries

Go to www.launchrock.com and check out its landing page template. Such a simple landing page. Over 7 million registrations. Takes five minutes to build your own. How can life be this easy?

Again, LaunchRock has shown that less is more, and sometimes big fancy elaborate squeeze pages can't beat the humble "coming soon" page. At a minimum, **you would be crazy** not to split test this against any other landing page you decide to come up with. Crazy, I tell ya.

Action Exercise 1: If you only had three sentences to describe your opt-in page, how would you do it?

Action Exercise 2: Try using a micro-squeeze page like LaunchRock, LeadPages, or building one yourself. Compare this to your current opt-in conversion rates.

Another Record Breaking Webinar Landing Page

I just started using LeadPages a few weeks ago to build some "quick and nasty" landing pages for campaigns where I just want to get things out the door quickly and not have to wait for a new landing page to be built. I gotta say, the platform is quite solid. It's got some limitations, but the positives (you can build a landing page without IT) outweigh the limitations.

I made contact with LeadPages to find out about some high-converting landing page templates they've created, and this one by Aussie online marketer James Schramko caught my eye:

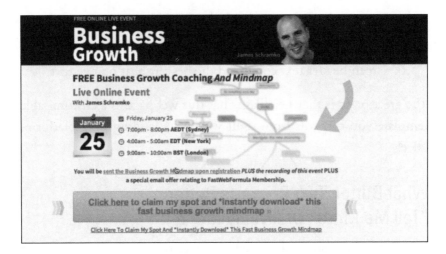

It's a different spin on your regular webinar landing page, and here's why:

1. There's no name and email box on the actual landing page; you click on the button and a pop-over appears where you can just enter your email address. This is good because it avoids people feeling like they're being "squeezed."

2. The blurred out view of the mindmap in the background makes you curious so you want to get it! Smart play, James.

3. It links directly to the GoToWebinar platform, so you don't need to enter your details twice to join the webinar. This is good because the GoToWebinar landing page looks as attractive as toilet water. And also, people get confused; they're like "Hey, I just registered already; what's this GoToWebinar form thingy?" And confused people don't generally enter their email addresses again.

4. James found that no bullets or sales copy on the landing page actually converted better than having bullets. Key lesson: Keep it simple. Don't overwrite the copy when you're just asking for a free opt-in.

5. And in the Call to Action box, when he took out the words "claim your," it actually doubled his conversions again. Les-

son: Don't get too cute with the wording; just let people know it's a free session and a free download.

6. Green header text converted the best. It beat orange text.

The great news is that LeadPages has this webpage as a customisable template you can edit from right within its landing page platform. Nice!

What Button Text Converts Better: "Tell Me More" Or "Notify Me"?

LeadPages was also kind enough to share the results of its "coming soon" split test.

The "coming soon" split test comes from Maggie Percy at discoveringdousing.com. What Maggie did is she split-tested the exact same page, except on one of the pages, the button text says, "tell me more." On the other page, the button text says, "notify me."

What she found was that the page that says "tell me more," out-converted the page that just says "notify me" by about 30 percent. In other words, there was a 30 percent relative increase when she used "tell me more" versus "notify me."

In Maggie's case, this goes to show that her audience was more interested in getting information than they were about getting notified when she launched. The reason why "tell me more" converts better is the urge to have more information is usually greater than the urge to be told the second something launches.

What Design Makes A Sales Page Convert?

Ask 100 marketers what makes a good sales page and you will get 100 different answers. As you know, this book is all about real life examples of stuff that is working out in the field right now. There are some designs that are "ugly ducklings"—and they convert like crazy! There are other designs that have won awards—but nobody buys from them. It's really something you need to test and measure for your business.

Because this area of marketing changes so quickly, the free book resources page (http://www.feedastarvingcrowd.com/resources) is always updated with the latest sales pages that are converting the best.

Four Simple Checkout Improvements Based On A Comprehensive Study Of 3,000 Examples

This is the most commonly missed part for online marketers. So much focus goes into the home page, the squeeze page, and the sales page that everyone always forgets about the poor old checkout. Depending on which research study you read, the shopping cart abandonment rate is generally between 60 to 80 percent. Even at the low-end, that means that out of every ten people who add something to the cart, six of them decide not to go ahead and buy the product from you.

If you compare that to an offline store, it's like six out of ten people bringing the product to the shopping counter and then turning away and saying, "Nah, I don't want this anymore." The poor old store manager would go crazy!

The saddest thing is that most businesses don't even measure their shopping cart abandonment rates.

So how do you avoid this calamity? You think through it very carefully, apply some best-practice principles, and then watch your sales improve. Here's the story of how we did it at E-Web Marketing for one of our clients.

In August, the last month of the old checkout process, our ecommerce conversion rate was 3.59 percent site-wide. That's pretty good for most websites. But we still weren't happy with it.

The original checkout process looked like this:

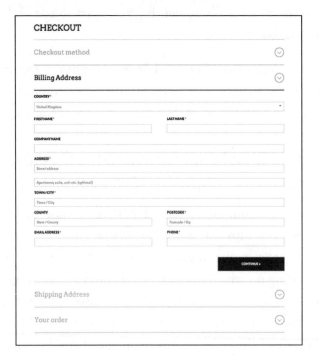

Beautiful right? Maybe not.

We had a couple of problems with this checkout:

1. It wasn't mobile friendly. The biggest problem was the conversion rate for mobile devices. It was sitting at a measly 0.89 percent when the average was at 3.59 percent. Something wasn't right.

2. We had forced user registration and required users to enter in a username and password. Again. Not ideal.

I decided to get out there and research what actually makes a best practice checkout. I mean, I'm supposed to be running a best-practice shop around here, right? In my research, I came across an excellent report from a company called Baymard Institute. These guys had done all the hard work already for me!

Baymard pulled up the top fifteen online stores (by revenue) and then completed a comprehensive usability study on each one of these stores. They got random users in a room and watched them as the users tried to buy products from each of these stores, so they could find out where the users got confused. From this research, they then wrote a large report with sixty-three guidelines for checkout usability.

We implemented these guidelines on this client's website, and our ecommerce conversion rate improved 18.7 percent across the board. Most importantly, our mobile conversions increased from 0.89 percent to 1.90 percent—we doubled our mobile revenue.

Here's the wireframes for a digital checkout:

And here's one extra screen you see only when your purchase needs to be delivered to a physical address:

Here were my biggest "aha" moments with best-practice checkouts:

1. Minimise the text that the user needs to type in at every stage. I was ruthless with this step for the new checkout. We went through every single field and questioned why we needed that information. I even negotiated with our payment provider not to require a billing address for digital-only products (saved five fields). Everything counts!

We've implemented auto-country detection based on IP address so the user doesn't have to choose a country. When the user enters his credit card information, we don't ask him to choose AMEX, Visa, or MasterCard; we just auto-detect the card based on the digits the user types in.

We were asking before for a phone number as a required field. But we very rarely had a reason to call our clients, and if we did, it wasn't that hard to ask for a phone number by email.

With all of these tiny little details, nobody is going to say, "Yeah, thanks for removing the billing address," but when you add all of these things up, it at least halves the time it takes for a user to complete your checkout. And the faster users gets through your checkout, the better for your wallet (because they won't get distracted and leave the site before completing payment).

2. Remove navigation once the user is in the checkout. Once the user has pressed "checkout," it's time to do business. Get rid of all the header navigation and footer navigation so your user can focus on completing the checkout without any distractions. Keep him focused!

3. Format the expiration date exactly as it appears on the credit card (e.g. 01/17). You'll see some inefficient checkouts that have you select the month and then the year, like February 2015. This is just plain confusing for people. There's the chance they'll get the calculation of 9/15 wrong and think it's August 2015 when it's really September 2015. Any errors users can make, they will!

4. Allow people to purchase in their home currency. For this client's website, we were always getting complaints from overseas people who didn't want to pay in Australian dollars; they wanted to pay in their home currency. So we set up the site to auto-detect the user's country, and offer different currencies for overseas buyers.

Baymard's report is excellent, and I highly recommend it to you if you'd like to take your checkout to the next level.

Action Exercise: Can you apply any of these best-practice checkout principles to your process?

Another Nifty Opt-In Feature If You're Doing A Lot Of Video Marketing

Most of E-Web Marketing's clients are using a lot of video in their marketing campaigns. There's so many reasons to use video, and the production cost is now microscopic compared to where it used to be.

If you're using a lot of free video tips as a marketing tool, my good friends over at Wistia have developed a neat little opt-in box that sits over the top of your video. So when the user enters his email, it unlocks the video. Here's what it looks like from one of E-Web's recent launches:

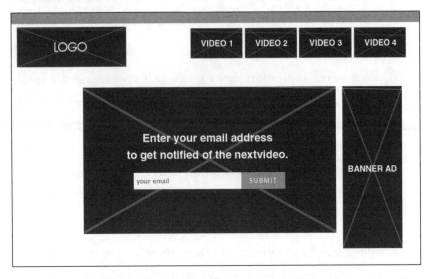

Action Exercise: If you do any video marketing, what can you do to ensure you capture your users' email addresses before allowing them access to your juicy content?

How We Halved The Cost Of Leads To Attend A Free Seminar

For one of our clients, we had the brief to fill up three seminar rooms of people who would be interested in investments. Sounds easy, right? Wrong!

The investor market is actually one of the most crowded and toughest markets to advertise online for. You're competing against a lot of investment advertisers with deep pockets and huge advertising budgets. You're also competing against savvy event promoters who are very switched on with online marketing and have tested and optimised many different traffic sources and landing pages.

So back to our campaign. From past experience, we have found that what works well is to point people to a landing page where they can watch a free video after entering their names and email addresses. Then on the "thank you" page, we invite them to come to the free seminar. The flow looks something like this:

This process is a very sensible strategy in theory. It's logical to assume you'll get a better conversion rate of people watching a free video because no matter where they are in the world, they would be interested in watching the video, and then from there, you can get them to register for the event either on the spot (woohoo!) or you can email market to them for registering later.

We started with this funnel, and it worked quite well, converting at 2.7 percent.

So we thought, "Let's try one more experiment and go directly to the registration page, cutting out all of this free video stuff...."

And boom! Conversion rate of 5.5 percent, halved the cost per lead. Way better!

Takeaway message: Don't assume anything! Test adding steps to the funnel, and test taking away steps from the funnel.

Action Exercise: Are there any steps you can take away from your funnel to test whether it then converts better?

BONUS TIP:
THE BEST WAY TO ADVERTISE ON MAJOR NEWS WEBSITES

News websites are one of the highest quality source of traffic going around. Problem is, they cost a fortune to advertise on. The good news is that there are new platforms which enable you to advertise on these sites for a very low cost per click. Visit the free book resources section for my latest recommendations: http://www.feedastarvingcrowd.com/resources

6

GETTING AFFILIATES, BLOGGERS, AND JOINT VENTURE PARTNERS ON BOARD—WHAT ACTUALLY WORKS TODAY

"It is rare to find a business partner who is selfless. If you are lucky it happens once in a lifetime."
— **Michael Eisner**

Joint ventures helped an investment company sell $500m of products in one year. Not bad for a single strategy! I explain how they did it later in this chapter. First I want to share some background information with you.

I've been approached to send email to the E-Web list by all types of businesses. One was a webinar training company, one was an email list broker, one was a email marketing/CRM platform, and one was an online video platform. All of these people thought that the E-Web database could potentially purchase their products. And I agreed with them and decided to interview them and share this information with the E-Web list.

Some campaigns went better than others. Some campaigns hit the ball out of the park. For other campaigns, we didn't even make one sale!

I've also been recommended to other people's lists as well. Sometimes we've done well; sometimes, we've sold nothing!

What I'm going to do in this chapter is analyse what has worked well for me with affiliate marketing, and also show you what some of the top people in the world are doing with affiliate marketing.

A strong affiliate network can take you a very long way to your million dollar launch.

Business owners have been forming joint ventures for hundreds of years, supporting each other by endorsing each other's products and services. The only thing that has changed today thanks to Internet technology is the speed and volume with which you can create and profit from joint venture (JV) partnerships.

JV experts Rich German and Milana Leshinsky claim that over 80 percent of businesses using JVs in their marketing mix go from zero to six and seven figures very fast. Is it really possible to achieve this incredible type of exponential growth?

Let's find out.

The logic behind the JV concept is grounded on the notion of synergy. Derived from the Greek word *sunergia* meaning "working together," synergy refers to the interaction of two or more cooperative agents or forces so that their combined effect is greater than the sum of their individual effects.

The JV game is very powerful if played well. In other words: **Cooperation, cooperation, and more cooperation.**

Where To Find Affiliate Marketers In The First Place

So the holy grail is to find a marketer who has a large list of subscribers in his database, who has a non-competing, complementary product to yours, who is happy to mail his subscribers recommending your stuff, and to whom you only pay a commission on any of the sales that come through.

How in the blue moon are you going to do this?

The simplest way is to look at who comes before, during, or after your product is purchased. For example, with our business of online marketing, before someone needs online marketing, he needs a website, hosting, and a domain name. All of these companies are natural JV partners for our business.

And after someone starts using online marketing and he starts making sales on his site, he is going to need order fulfillment, shipping, video production, public relations, and a whole bunch of other stuff.

Any of these types of businesses are not competitive to ours, and they also improve the lives of the customer. If a customer is having major issues with his warehouse and shipping, it means he will want to slow down his online marketing because he can't keep up with the demand. So if we can get him to start using a world-class fulfillment company, then it's a win-win all round.

Action Exercise: The common sense approach here is to put yourself in your potential JV partner's shoes. If you had a solid list of subscribers, and someone wanted you to promote him, what five questions would you ask?

1. _____

2. _____

3. _____

4. _____

5. _____

Here are some more ways to find JVs:

1. Bookstores, online and off. Authors of books in your field are always looking to expand their reach and boost their exposure.

2. Social media pages. Pay attention not only to contributors but also to people who leave comments.

3. Search engines and alerts. Do a search using your keywords to find potential JV partners. Set up Google Alerts and receive news from your industry daily or weekly. Some names will come up often. These are the people you need to look out for: article writers, blog directories, online forums, and groups. The major contributors in these types of spaces are trying to prove their expertise and ever-willingness to help. Pick a few and look them up.

4. Specialised online platforms dedicated to establishing contacts among potential JV partners, including 1000 legs and JV Billboard. (Note: There are links to these online platforms and more in the free book resources section: http://www.feed-astarvingcrowd.com/resources.)

5. You can also look at your suppliers: Information marketer Yanik Silver explains he entered into a JV with a telemarketer to whom he paid a large percentage of sales for events and other high-end products he was producing. This joint venture brought him millions of dollars in extra revenue, Yanik says. Instead of hiring employees and running a mail shop himself, Yanik gets all his direct-mail marketing done on a joint venture basis: "My partner does all the little things necessary to get a direct-mail piece out," he explains. "He's also a good copywriter, so he writes envelope teasers, lift notes, and so on, too. I pay him based on the results of each mailing. We are both in it together. If I do well, so does he."

Action Exercise: Your action exercise for this part is really easy. Make a list of potential joint venture partners. What complementary businesses come before, during, or after your product or service?

1. _____

2. _____

3. _____

4. _____

5. _____

What's Possible With Joint Ventures— How Jay Abraham Boosted A Company's Revenue By $500m With No Paid Advertising

Jay Abraham is one of the world's top marketing consultants. He charges $5,000 per hour. I'm not sure if you'd engage in a lot of small talk for that kind of fee!

Jay is well-known for being an expert in joint ventures and affiliate relationships. When he first started doing joint ventures, one of his first clients was a gold and silver brokerage firm. It sold coins, bars, gold, stocks, and silver. It was running newspaper and magazine ads and doing all right.

Jay thought he could help the firm do better. He found all the complementary businesses to this brokerage firm—businesses who had a relationship with people who already understand and appreciate buying gold.

Jay approached financial newsletters and magazines, authors who sold books on investing, and seminar companies who sell investments. These companies didn't sell gold, but a high percentage of their target markets did buy gold.

Jay formed partnerships with these complementary companies. They would promote the brokerage firm in return for a commission on sales. The brokerage firm did pretty well from this arrangement. $500 Million In One Year From That One Strategy. Not Bad At All.

Approaching Affiliate Partners, Making Sure Your Proposal Stands Out From The Others, And Getting Them To Say, "Yes"

My friend Simone Novello runs a company called PartnerUp. All day, every day, she helps people make joint ventures. I asked for her top tips on how to approach potential partners and she had some excellent advice.

She shared the following approach template that has been used to seal deals in the real world!

Hello Caroline,

Simone suggested I give you a call as she thinks there might be some synergies we should explore to benefit both our businesses.

I am an online organic gardening teacher and artist and my target market are 35-50 year old busy women with children who are health conscious.

I'd love to offer you my Organic Gardening planner valued at $14.95 as a gift so you can experience my work.

Would you be free for a coffee next week to discuss potential opportunities for mutual benefit?

Kind regards, Nicola

Simone also shared some great ways to approach people using LinkedIn, email, and phone:

LinkedIn

NEVER send a generic connect request. Use LinkedIn InMail or at least see whether you have a common connection and reference it in the connect request. Mention same target market and synergies.

Email

Some people don't check LinkedIn often so you may wish to send a short email if you have an email address. Keep it succinct, try to make a warm reference, and mention the same target market and synergies.

Phone

Don't expect them to call you back—ALWAYS follow up with a phone call (about 1-2 weeks after you've made initial contact).

Being confident helps massively when you're calling.

I learnt a lot about cold calling from many different teachers. I can safely say that the number one authority on cold calling was Chet Holmes. Unfortunately, he's passed away, but I was fortunate to capture some of his top tips for getting through to executives. Using these tactics, I've been able to cold call and score meetings with senior executives of large corporations and government departments just by being confident.

Some of his top tips are:

1. You need to convey authority. End your sentences on a "down note."

2. Take your time; don't let the executive rush you.

3. Answer the gatekeepers' questions in advance: "Hi, this is Robert Coorey; is Peter Smith in?" (Act like Peter is expecting your call and there's a good chance the gatekeeper will put you straight through).

4. When asked, "What's this in regards to?" reply, "Tell him I'm with E-Web." (Again, convey authority.)

Also, when you are making phone calls, there's a huge chance you'll be put into voicemail. It's a real pain. But let me tell you something: Executives check their voicemail! A lot of them don't read their emails, but they definitely check voicemail. They also check SMS.

A Great Success Story

Being extremely busy people, your potential partners will *not* even glance at your proposition if it doesn't stand out from the pack. Often a product has great potential, but it will get passed over because your JV did not capture the prospective partner's eye at first sight. So, if you need to go as far as Australian Entrepreneur Pete Williams did, you might actually get the same kind of response he did.

Pete had an idea to build an iPhone app, which he eventually called Openers (or conversation starters). So you open up the iPhone app, shake it, and it produces for you a good opening conversation line. Pete tested it to see how it went in terms of actual penetration and response and then put together a pitch. He then approached a potential JV person with whom he had a remote connection, being friends of a friend. He had a name to drop, a kind of an endorsement.

But this is what Pete did: He put together a seven slide PowerPoint presentation with some sketches of what the application would look like, how it would work, some numbers, and how the actual JV could be structured as an idea. He put the PowerPoint presentation on his computer screen, grabbed screen-recording software and just talked through this presentation—a kind of Video Sales Letter (check the section in Chapter 9 on VSLs). In the end, he made a short video that covered all the important points. He emailed the link to his potential JV partner, saying, "Hey, I've got an idea for an iPhone app. I put together a quick video overview of how I think it could work. Buzz me back if you think it's interesting."

Twelve minutes later, he got a reply: "Love the idea. Was blown away by the presentation."

Pete's approach was fresh, different; it wasn't a thirty-page sales pitch. It stood out. It was unique. He actually built a prototype, was knowledgeable about the industry, and it got him some of those real numbers so he could give them to his potential partner. All he needed was an innovative way to approach him. A winning formula. He presented a package—the numbers, the proposal, the app design—in a way the potential partner had immediate access to and even was able to share with other colleagues.

And if it all doesn't work out once, twice, ten times, don't take rejection personally. Don't ever send back an angry email if you hope to work with that person. That will immediately flag you as a potentially bad partner, further justifying your rejection. JVs can sometimes take time, and sometimes, you have to go through a few nay's before you get a yay.

Action Exercise: Choose one or two ways to approach affiliates and give it a crack!

How To Find An Affiliate Manager To Sign Up The Affiliates For You

I'm one of those guys who finds it hard to let go of control. I've been the one typically who has reached out and organised the affiliate deals. If you're not keen to do this yourself, Jay Abraham recommends you run an advertisement to get an affiliate manager on board:

> Looking for current or ex-salespeople who have a great rela-
> tionship with their past or current clients to represent our joint
> venturing business, full or part-time. Could do this while you
> keep your other job. A profit share for life. Contact me.

The point is, whether you do it yourself or hire someone else to do it,
joint ventures can be awesome for your business.

Simple But Little-Known Tips On How To Negotiate The Best Profit Split

I learnt an awesome negotiation tactic from business coach Andrew
Roberts. Andrew has set up a stack-load of affiliate deals, and he
starts with offering an iPad in return for you emailing your list for
him. And that's not a bad deal—for a $500 iPad, you're getting your
deal blasted to 1,000, or 10,000, or maybe even 50,000 people.

Before you dismiss that tactic, Andrew has done a lot of these. Many
people who have a decent database are not in the Internet marketing
community. They don't realise that the going rate for an affiliate marketing commission can be 50 percent or more. So you don't have to
go out there and give away 50 percent of your profit upfront. You're
better off starting low with an iPad, and then negotiating from there.

Andrew then moves up to 10 percent, 25 percent, and finally, 50
percent if it's a savvy online marketer with a huge list. Great strategy.

Recognising Reputable Affiliates

You want to be careful here. Some affiliates don't do the right thing.
If you're promoting someone else's product, the risk you run is that
he won't pay you! I've had this happen a few times before, and you
need to be street-smart to make sure you get paid for your hard work.

On the flip side, if someone else is promoting your product, you
want to make sure he doesn't have any misleading sales copy or mis-

represent your product! He might say your product can do X when it can't really, just so he can make the sale.

I don't mean to put a damper on affiliate marketing, but you need to be aware of the potential pitfalls of joint ventures to make sure you don't get screwed over.

How do I avoid all these pitfalls?

1. I try to collect the cash whenever possible.

2. If I can't collect the cash, I'll make sure the affiliate has a custom product setup, with a custom sales page, etc., so there's no confusion over which affiliate sent the traffic.

3. If someone is selling our stuff, we will send him "swipe copy" so the copy correctly represents the product.

Good affiliates are always wanting to know the answers to these questions:

- Have your results been proven?

- Do you have testimonials from the people your product has benefited?

- Is your sales page/video tested and converting well?

- Do you have a personable and effective customer support system in place?

- Do you have a quality follow-up process to convert prospects into customers?

- Is your intention first to help others, not just to make more sales of your product?

- Are you capable of presenting your ideas and over-delivering value regardless of what you get in return?

Action Exercise: Create good answers for these questions, so affiliates will be more inclined to mail for you.

How To Get Affiliates ACTUALLY To Mail For You

Here is another pitfall of affiliates (I hope I haven't scared you off!)....

So the affiliate has agreed to email its list promoting your product, and then....silence. The affiliate doesn't actually send the email. You get in touch and ask politely when the affiliate will be sending it, and silence. The affiliate stops answering your emails and doesn't return your phone calls. It's like he's turned into Batman!

And you know he's still around because he's emailing everyone else's damn offers, but not yours!

Don't laugh; this is a very common occurrence. Many affiliates get cold feet before they are due to do a mailing, so they don't proceed.

How do you make sure your affiliates ACTUALLY hit send on their email marketing platforms and spread the good news about your stuff to their universes?

Well, there are two ways to get someone to do anything—there's the carrot and there's the stick. On a side note, a carrot and a stick are the two ways you motivate a donkey to walk. You either put a carrot in front of it and it moves forward to eat the carrot, or you whack it with a stick from behind (poor donkey).

With online marketing and affiliates, a stick is not going to do you any good. You have no authority to apply the stick to an affiliate.

The only hope you have is to make that carrot so damn juicy and appealing that the affiliate will jump over any obstacle to get your carrot.

Now, getting practical, the simplest way is to make the incentives so high that affiliates are actually *excited* to email their list for you. The top Internet marketers do this so well. Have you ever seen an Eben Pagan launch or a Jeff Walker launch where it seems that every man and his dog, and his dog's dog, is emailing you to go and buy his stuff? It's because they're using these tactics I'm about to share with you.

Tactic #1—Keep a public leaderboard of the top affiliates

Most top Internet marketers are extremely competitive and want to win. They want to see how good they are compared to the others, and then they want to do whatever it takes to come first.

Here's what a standard leaderboard looks like:

Tactic 2—Affiliate prizes

EasyVideo Suite recently did a million dollar launch, and its prizes were quite attractive. I mean, who wouldn't want to mail their list hard to get the Turkey and Greece tour?

1st Place: Travel Turkey & Greece Tour to the value of $15,000, OR the cash equivalent of $15,000

2nd Place: Luxurious Liner Cruise of the Caribbean to the value of $7000, OR the cash equivalent of $7000

3rd Place: Train Travel West to East USA to the value of $5000, OR the cash equivalent of $5000

4th Place: California Wine Tours to the value of $3000, OR the cash equivalent of $3000

5th Place: iPhone 5 + iPad (4th Gen.) + GoPro Hero 3 Black Edition, OR the cash equivalent of $1500

Tactic 3—Big commissions

The going rate for digital information products is 50 percent because you have no variable cost. Physical products are usually in the 10 to 25 percent range because of the shipping and handling fees.

What Eben Pagan did really well for his accelerate launch was to offer a $50,000 cash prize to the top affiliate, and to double this cash prize if the affiliate sent out all four launch videos. So the affiliates were all competing for a potential $100,000 payday, plus the commission for selling the course. Very exciting prizes, just for sending a few emails to your list!

Tactic 4—Run a customised webinar to an affiliate's list

A customised webinar to an affiliate's list will ensure that affiliates mail their lists and their followers will turn up. It is also one of the most powerful ways to promote your product. If you can get some-one to sit in front of his computer for an hour and listen to your pitch, you've got a good chance to close a deal, right?

Running webinars to lists has been my primary method of affiliate marketing. In the Internet marketing community, webinars are get-ting a bit old. In other niches, many people still don't even know what a webinar is, so you need to use different wording. My friend

Alexi recommends using the term "online seminar." When I heard that for the first time, it actually blew my mind and made me angry at the same time. I was happy that someone had pointed out the blindingly obvious to me, but I was also annoyed that I had wasted so many leads in the past because I was using the wrong language.

Affiliate marketers have many different methods at their disposal:

- Email blast to their lists

- PPC traffic

- Dedicated webinar to their lists

- Special content just for their lists (BRW subscription comp)

- Exclusive "early bird" registration for their lists

- Customised bonus from the affiliate when people on their lists buy your product

Which ones do you want them using? Actually, all of them!

If I had to choose just one, I would choose the customised bonus from the affiliate when someone buys your product. As an example, during Eben's launch, Jeff Walker even offered to give you his phone number to call and do one-on-one consulting (which he hadn't done in seven years).

All I can say is WOW.

Action Exercise: How can you offer something so compelling that the prospect would be crazy to turn down your bonus?

Ultimate Lessons I've Learnt From One Of The World's Top Affiliate Marketers

Getting your affiliates to blast their lists can sometimes be as hard as pushing a tractor uphill. First, you need to get the affiliate to agree to blast his list, and then he's actually got to load up the email in the client and hit "send."

Most marketing gurus will claim that it's really easy to get affiliates to mail. I've seen claims like "just build relationships with JV partners and they'll be happy to mail for you." Great! Try doing that in the real world.

In keeping with the theme of this book, I'm only presenting to you strategies and tactics that actually work. So for this section, I interviewed one of the world's top experts in affiliate marketing, Dush Ramachandran from The Net Momentum.

The Net Momentum is a company that recruits and manages affiliates for you when you want to sell lots of product. It does a lot of other things as well, but in this chapter, we'll focus on the affiliate management side of its business.

Prior to The Net Momentum, Dush served as Vice President of Sales and Business Development at ClickBank where he was responsible for substantially growing the company's revenues in less than six years. His wife Terra, who originally founded the business, created and implemented the ClickBank Apex and Premier programs. These programs recognized and rewarded ClickBank's top 500 vendors and affiliates.

Just in the last two years, The Net Momentum has created over $15 million in affiliate revenue.

So these guys know what they're talking about.

Dush's team performs the online equivalent of "wearing out shoe leather" as a salesperson would on the street. The team will contact all the affiliates to make sure they are promoting your product, lock down the dates when they will mail, and follow up to make sure that mailing actually happens, and the team will get a constant revenue stream flowing to you from as many affiliates as possible.

Dush shared some real gold when I spoke to him. And now I am going to share that gold with you.

Always Personalize Your Pitch For The Big Hitters

Sending a generic affiliate request to a big hitter is a guaranteed recipe for disaster. The big hitters have massive calendars full of email promotions that are booked out for three months in advance. Why would they even bother reading an unsolicited template email from someone they don't know?

Dush recommends you take the time to understand the company's business and show how your product is complementary to what it sells.

Recently, while recruiting affiliates for one of his health and fitness clients who has a diet product, Dush focused on people who offer other health products and supplements. But he also included someone who is selling a product that teaches users how to improve their golf games.

Now hang on a second—how does golf training correspond to a diet product?

In this case, Dush customized the pitch to emphasize the fact that in order to be truly effective at golf, you need to be in good physical shape. Dush suggested to the vendor that his users were more likely to achieve better results with his golf product if they were in better shape, and therefore, if he were to promote the diet product, his users might get more value from his golf product. This resulted in a very successful promotion.

Interestingly, Dush won't take every offer to each affiliate on his database. He'll only present offers that he feels are a natural fit for an affiliate's existing following. This is counterintuitive to the normal "spray and pray" approach of blasting everyone about every deal, hoping for the best.

And if you can manage to land a big whale, the results can be extremely exciting. Dush reports big hitters can send upwards of 25,000 clicks to your sales page if they really get behind an offer.

Don't Forget About The Small Guys

Dush mentioned that many people only focus on the top big hitters for each category and forget about the small guys—the thousands of smaller affiliates who are happy to mail hard on your behalf. Dush said that when you add up all the small guys, it can far exceed the revenue from the big guys. The small guys are easier to get on board, will mail more often, and will push harder for you than the big guys.

It can be a challenge to keep the small guys interested and engaged throughout the launch. Think about it from their perspective. If you're a small guy with a list of 5,000 people, and the big guys are hammering their 1,000,000+ lists with big bonuses, what chance do you have of winning any of the affiliate prizes or showing up in the Top 10 on the leaderboard?

Lucky for us, Dush has thought about this problem.

To keep the small guys engaged, he says, you gamify the process. And instead of just giving out a commission on revenue, you create a points system. So every time affiliates mail, they get points. If they create a testimonial and send it through—they get points. If you call up our affiliate manager and tell us a joke—you get points. If you wake up in the morning and jump out of bed—you get points.

Okay, maybe not the last one—but you get the point.

So, obviously, the big guys aren't going to ring your affiliate manager and tell a joke, but the small guys will! And remember, when you add up the revenue from all the rats and mice, it can be more than the revenue from the big guys.

Think About Evergreen Revenue After The Launch

Dush is a master at maximizing revenue during the launch, as well as keeping an evergreen affiliate revenue stream going post-launch. I could understand how he gets the launch revenue in the door, but how can you continue to make revenue from affiliates post-launch? Isn't it all over once they stop blasting?

Apparently not. Dush has organized integrations of products into affiliates' back end systems—so that when someone buys product A from an affiliate, he gets an upsell to buy your product B after the purchase. So that can be a solid perpetual revenue stream for your business. Dush has also arranged for affiliates to place special offers for your product in their members' area, so every time a new customer logs in, he sees an offer for your product. Brilliant.

For smaller affiliates, another tactic you can use is only to sign them up post-launch, so you've got different affiliates promoting at different times. This balances out your revenue stream and provides consistent income over a longer period of time.

One last trick with the small affiliates—Dush actually trains these guys only to send qualified traffic.

I wondered why he would go to the trouble to do that—shouldn't you be encouraging your affiliates to send any sort of traffic they can get their hands on?

Turns out that not all traffic is good traffic.

If a small affiliate sends you buckets of unqualified traffic that does not buy, it ruins your earnings-per-click statistics, and that makes it harder for the big guys to sign up and sell your product.

Dush found that smaller affiliates for a weight loss supplement were not being as effective as they could be in advertising through social media. The target market for this particular supplement is mostly women in their thirties and forties. Dush suggested to the affiliates that they might try using Pinterest, where the user demographic is predominantly female. Dush's team trained them on how they could pin an infographic to Pinterest, which would attract the interest of the target demographic. This infographic would then be repinned, and then picked up and repinned again and again, going viral in the process. Embedding an affiliate sales link in the infographic allows a huge number of people in the target demographic to be exposed to the message. This Pinterest strategy was not very well-known, so it resulted in great results for the affiliate and the vendor. I also cover a lot more Pinterest strategies in Chapter 7.

How Do You Get The Big Guys To Say "Yes"

To get the big guys to say, "Yes," here are the bare minimum requirements you'll need:

1. A proven conversion rate and high Earnings Per Click, or EPC (EPC refers to how much the affiliate will make for every click it sends to your offer)

2. All of the affiliate tools ready to go—banner ads, email swipe copy, videos, frequently asked questions, you're available to interview on webinar

3. A unique product that offers enormous value

4. They need to trust that you're legitimate and not going out of business tomorrow

5. Your offer needs to be more appealing to knock off one of their existing scheduled affiliate mailings! For one of his Forex trading clients, Dush organized a massive affiliate party in Vegas for the top fifty affiliates, which was well-attended. I mean— who wouldn't want to hang out at a cool party in Vegas?

6. If you're brand new and have no track record, it might be an idea to work with an affiliate manager like The Net Momen-

tum. Affiliate managers already have all of the relationships and contacts in place, and when they take on a project, it gives you that extra bit of credibility. A solid affiliate manager could be the difference between whether or not your affiliate launch gets off the ground.

Leading "Mum Blogger" Shows Three Simple Outreach Strategies That Actually Work To Get Blog Coverage

Fiona Purcell is a very successful Australian "Mummy blogger" who not only has her own loyal following of fans, but she also has a great network of other bloggers whom she organises for blogger events and brand marketing activities. Fiona has been approached thousands of times as part of a "blogger outreach" strategy by marketers. She was even invited to lunch by the former Australian Prime Minister Julia Gillard (nice!). Below she shares some great examples of what works and what doesn't work:

Working with bloggers is a fantastic way to share your brand message. Personal bloggers share their personal thoughts, real feelings, and relatable experiences with their readers across multiple platforms. It is because of this honesty that bloggers are able to build a loyal and trusting relationship with their readership.

Take a Mum Blogger for example. Her audience learns humorous and intimate details of her day-to-day life as a mother. She may share her frustrations with toilet training, her anguish over balancing work-life with motherhood, her struggle with post-natal depression, or the jubilation of fitting into her pre-pregnancy jeans. Her readers come to see this mother as their friend, and they feel that they "know" her and her family from following her story online.

If this Mum Blogger were to endorse your brand or product on her blog or social media platforms, it would carry a greater influence than some other advertising mediums. This is because of the trusting, friend-like relationship she has with her readers, regardless of the size of her audience.

This may sound simple in theory, but it is not as fool-proof in practice. There's some important do's and don'ts to consider before initiating your own Blogger Outreach strategy.

1. You need a hook. PR events are a great way to get bloggers together to interact and start talking on their social media platforms about your brand and/or product. However, one of the challenges in this blogger outreach strategy is getting influential bloggers to attend your event. Events can take a lot of time out of a blogger's day, and when invitations are coming thick and fast, you need to have a hook to entice them there.

   Scenario:

   The launch of a new beauty range

   Bad event—A public launch with guests from mainstream media being handed press releases and gift bags.

   Good event—An intimate lunch with a high-profile guest, including a pamper session for each blogger using the new beauty range.

2. Be personal. A personal blog is not a magazine or news agency. Sending a press release, a generic email, or anything beginning with 'Dear Blogger' is not going to cut it. Effective blogger outreach is about developing a connection with the bloggers you want to work with. Taking the time to connect with a smaller group of bloggers is going to be far more effective than sending out a generic, impersonal email and hoping for the best.

   Scenario: ABC Childrenswear would like to connect with the audiences of personal bloggers

Bad email—"Hi there, ABC, Childrenswear is launching its brand new label this week. This is a fantastic range that we just know your readers will love! Please find our press release attached and be in touch if you would like to feature this label on your site. Kind Regards, Bronwyn"

Good email—"Hi, Kate, how are your gorgeous boys doing? My name's Bronwyn from XYC Marketing. I loved your post last week about convincing your boys to wash their hair! I was wondering if you would be interested in the boys trialing some clothes from the new ABC Childrenswear label. I'd love to send a few outfits through and perhaps we could arrange a sponsored post on your lovely blog. Looking forward to hearing your thoughts, Bron"

3. It's all about the Win-Win-Win. A personal blog is a unique medium, certainly worthy of sharing your brand message. But before you pitch to the blogger, stop and think: What's in it for the blogger? What's in it for their readers? You may think your product is amazing, and it may be, but nothing is worth sharing unless the blogger and her audience is receiving value out of the arrangement. "Great content" is not a win.

Scenario: A toy company is introducing a new range ahead of Christmas

Bad offering—A press release accompanied with photographs of the toy range are mass-emailed to bloggers for inclusion in Christmas gift guides that they may be publishing.

Good offering—The children of targeted bloggers receive a toy each from the new range, and each blogger is given a shopping voucher to spend online, as well as a shopping voucher to offer to their readers in a giveaway.

Blogger Outreach, when harnessed well, can bring tremendous exposure for your brand, and lead to mutually-beneficial, long-term relationships with influential bloggers.

If you're keen on doing a blogger outreach campaign, I'd highly recommend hiring Fiona to take care of this for you. Her website is http://www.mymummydaze.blogspot.com.au/

How A New York Times Best-Selling Author Used Blogger Outreach

Tim Ferriss explains in his blog that before launching *The 4-Hour Workweek*, he spent his entire book launch's budget attending tech conferences getting to know bloggers at Mashable, Tech Crunch, Gizmodo, and other tech blogs targeted at the audience Ferriss hoped to reach. He formed genuine relationships with them. Being as clear as he is on his audience—"20 to 35 year-old tech savvy males with disposable income and an interest in hacking"—Ferriss invested a lot of time developing bona fide friendships with the online gatekeepers of his audience. He became a relationship-building machine.

He had no doubt—it was all about the trust factor.

"You need to develop relationships early," Tim explains. "Find the people with whom you share common interests, the people you would actually be good friends with and hang out and have beers with…and develop a legitimate friendship with them." Because the thing is "people don't care how good your idea is. People don't care how good your book is," Ferriss insists. "People want to know if they can trust you…they need to trust the messenger before they can even start to listen to the message."

But how did Tim become a trusted resource in the field of lifestyle design, fitness, weight loss, and gastronomy? Can he possibly be an expert in all these different fields at once?

That's debatable. But what he did was start a blog around the topic of lifestyle design and developed interesting, captivating, and thought-worthy content. The quality of his posts and his unique style of writing soon attracted an interested, dynamic community of people who in no time began to look to Tim as their leader; they believed in his concept, and they were curious and wanted to learn more about Tim's lifestyle design concept.

Trust Had Been Born

The media started to pick up on this connection and to notice the many people who seemed to trust Tim with a new trend. Soon enough, they couldn't wait to cover the topic and the book, particularly after Barnes & Noble decided to boycott Tim's book—because of Tim's exclusive publishing deal with Amazon.

Tim also worked on forming genuine, one-to-one relationships with like-minded people in new media sources—"I'd rather put my eggs in the basket of passionate, interesting and unique online content creators (than on traditional media sources). People that have a genuine relationship with their community. People that actually give a crap." Plus, his philosophy is, even if you ignore them, as soon as they hear the buzz, traditional media will come rushing to get coverage. "There becomes a point where they just can't ignore you."

And he was absolutely right. This is the list of traditional media outlets that covered Tim's launches:

- **USA Today**—'4-Hour' author Timothy Ferriss returns as a chef

- **The New York Times**—Fête Accompli | 4-Hour Feasting

- **The Wall Street Journal**—'4-Hour' Man Masters Food, The Good Life

- **Bon Appétit**—A Bird in the Pan: Testing "The 4-Hour Chef"

- **Outside Magazine**—From Modern to Mallman (one of three online, also a print piece)

- **CBS This Morning (Charlie Rose, Gayle King)**—Timothy Ferriss talks food, life lessons

- **WNYC**—The 4-Hour Chef: Lengthy Book Offers Short Cut to Kitchen Excellence

- **Fox & Friends**—'Recipe' for Success

- **The New York Post**—Required Reading

- **Dr. Oz**—Health-boosting Secrets From The 4-Hour Chef Tim Ferriss (almost an hour total on TV, plus online)

Remarkable.

But even more remarkable is the list of blogs, partners, and YouTube reviewers who went out of their way to promote *The 4-Hour Chef* simply as a result of the close bond Tim had earlier consolidated (see end of this chapter). Tim used the soft-sell (as opposed to hard-sell) strategy of the digital age at its best—a strategy that is a lot more involved than what it seems, but it's also a lot more rewarding.

So How Do You Replicate Tim's Path To Mega Success?

Bloggers.

Bloggers will help you get your audience in a state of hype. Quickly. Inexpensively. For the long-term. (And please remember, no interns and no templates! The moment a blogger senses you are using a template, you are gone. Not a chance.)

Content is generally your best bet as bloggers need lots of quality content tailor-made for their audiences. Guest posts not only help your search engine rankings, but they will also help build your brand name and send direct traffic to your site. There are other options—

you might want to be creative and pre-sign them up for a membership or buy their tickets to a conference you're sponsoring.

Whatever it is, you need to be able to stand out.

Ferriss' recommendation is to personalise the pitch to online bloggers and YouTube channel owners across all verticals:

- Food Enthusiasts

- Male Lifestyle

- Science + Tech Bloggers

- Mom Bloggers

- Lifehackers

For example, Tim spoke to Mom Bloggers about the food part in the book, and to the Lifehackers about the life experiments he did.

Tim provided a wealth of assets to be used: exclusive excerpts, interviews with Tim (live or recorded), his video book trailers and images.

Getting Attention From Bloggers

Use the subject line to get the attention of a blogger by making a reference to something very particular about his or her blog: "content suggestion for [blog title]." This type of subject line tends to get the blogger's attention because he or she is at least a little curious about what this email has to say about his or her particular post or even the blog in general. It also shows that you are not a spammer and didn't just email a hundred webmasters with the same email template.

The social media tool Buffer built its entire business on blogger outreach. It went from 0 to 100,000 customers for its product in nine months using guest posting only. Leo Widrich, the co-founder and writer of Buffer, wrote 150 guest posts in this time, using MyBlog-Guest and BloggerLinkUp to find guest blogging opportunities.

Later on, Leo just emailed the bigger sites directly, finding the contributions editors and getting in touch.

How do you think of topics to write? Simple—find posts on other sites that already have heaps of comments, Likes, and shares, and put your own unique spin on them!

Buffer measures guest blogging by the amount of visitor referral traffic it gets from an article. Its goal is to get at least 100 visits from an article, and at a 2 percent conversion rate, with a lifetime value of $220/user, it'll make $440 a post.

Blogger outreach is not always a guaranteed path to millions of dollars, though.

Travel writer Adam Costa scored fifty guest blog articles all to go live on the same day (which took three months of haggling!). He even got heavy hitting sites like ProBlogger, BusinessInsider, and Lifehacker to get on board.

He used a very simple approach, saying he was a fan of the site and named a specific blog post he liked. Costa then shared a few guest post suggestions and other posts he'd published. Finally, he assured the blog owner that the post would be submitted fully formatted with images, which saves the blog owner time and effort. (Blog owners are typically very busy and can't be bothered to format documents into their content management system—who blames them?)

After one week, he then wrote a follow-up email, which he estimates an additional 50 percent extra guest blog posts scored. Most people would think you could probably retire on the traffic and sales you'd get back from landing all fifty guest posts!

Unfortunately, it didn't work out that well for Adam.

ProBlogger was his biggest traffic win with 156 visits. I know; that's not a typo: only 156 visits.

In total, Adam got 1,019 referral visits for the first week from all of those fifty guest blogs (average of twenty visits per guest blog).

Somewhat underwhelming....

I had a look at his work and I think I know what went wrong.

Adam runs a travel site, called Trekity, that gives travel ideas to women. Great niche. However, many of the blogs that Adam wrote for were not travel sites. And a lot of the topics he wrote about had to do with marketing, not necessarily travel.

It's a pretty big ask to get people from business blogs to read an article about marketing, then to click-through to your travel website, and then make a transaction.

He did well to get 1,000 visits, considering the hurdles people needed to jump through to make that connection.

In summary, guest blogging and blogger outreach can be awesome, but make sure you track your results carefully and adjust your strategy if it's not delivering the results.

Action Exercise: It's time for you to get coverage by bloggers. Make a list of ten bloggers, approach them, and get coverage!

1. _____   6. _____

2. _____   7. _____

3. _____   8. _____

4. _____   9. _____

5. _____   10. _____

7

USING LITTLE-KNOWN SOCIAL MEDIA SECRETS AND THINGS NOBODY ELSE IS DOING

"Social media is one area of business where you don't need to outspend your competitors in order to beat them."
— **Hal Stokes**

Social media is a funny beast. There is so much conjecture. Does it convert, or doesn't it convert? Can you sell on social, or is it wrong to sell on social? How can you measure your ROI for social?

Look, I'm just going to cut through the rubbish and give you the facts. Social sells. In this chapter, I will show you example after example of companies who have made money on social. You will see step-by-step exactly what they did. If the company has a big fan base and a starving crowd—how did it do it? If it ran a campaign that turned into leads or dollars, how did it do that?

You're going to learn exact how-tos. No fluff words like "build a community," "engage your audience," "make relationships" and "post often." None of that fluff!

And one more disclaimer. The world of social media changes so fast that the rules always change. That means what is working right now might not work tomorrow. I encourage you to stay in touch with the latest through the free book resources page.

How A "No-Name" Yoga Teacher Got More Than 1 Million Fans And Sold $1.5m In Revenue Through Facebook

Bret Gregory has created multiple Facebook pages, each with more than 200,000 fans, and he has closed over $1.5 million in sales from Facebook. The interesting thing is that most of this revenue has been in sales to attend his Yoga Retreat in Costa Rica. Interesting. Most yoga retreats I know are lucky to get ten people to pay anything! Bret's retreats are consistently booked out. He spends no money on advertising. And he spends five minutes a day on Facebook posting photos. Go figure.

Of course, I asked him to share his best tips on how to grow massive numbers of fans and convert those fans into paying customers. His top two techniques are the "photo stack" and the "article stack." I follow most top social media experts, but I had never heard of these two techniques before. These are good. Really good.

Photo Stack

Most businesses upload photos to their timelines, add descriptions, and hope for the best. Bret has a better way. You create a single album, and you keep uploading photos into this one album. When you do this, the likes for the album have a cumulative effect, so they will keep growing and growing. In the example below, Bret had 17,548 likes, 3,782 shares, and 393 comments on his photo stack—massive social proof.

Bret recommends adding nine photos at a time so that it presents like a nicely formatted 3x3 box.

After adding photos to a photo stack, Bret will normally get 200 to 600 new fans each time!

One more thing about the photo stack. It's best to write a description of the photos. Right underneath the photos, it says, "say something about this photo..." and that's where you write in the caption.

Getting People From Facebook To Your Website

Set up a "photo of the day" page on your website. This will have the same photos as your photo album stack. Include this URL in the description every time you post photos to your photo-stack on Facebook.

Now, the most critical thing here is to put only one Facebook Like button on your website. A big mistake people make when they're loading content on their websites is that each post, whether it's an article or a photo, has its own Like button. Well, when you do that, each Like button will start its count at zero.

You'll be starting over every time.

So what Bret recommends instead is to put one Like button for the entire album so every time you post a photo to the album or new photos to the album, you can share the URL of that album on your Facebook wall. Every time new people come to your website from Facebook and they click the Like button, you will then have the cumulative effect of Likes.

And the more Likes—the more social proof.

Bret credits this technique with driving 15,000 fans a month from Facebook to his website, just with the photo of the day stack.

You'd do well to learn more about Facebook marketing from Bret. He's got a lot of great information on his website—www.attractcustomer-snow.com. There's plenty of free tips, and he also runs live events to teach you his strategies in more detail. Highly recommended.

Action Exercise: Make sure you have a "Photo stack" online so your social proof stacks up.

Scientific Study Of 7,000 Facebook Posts Reveals The Two Factors Of A Viral Facebook Post

Punnky (Facebook.com/punnkydotcom) stands for Positive Uplifting News Network—started up by E-Web Marketing in November 2012. We started it as a way to share positive stories and inspirational quotes on a daily basis. We had no idea whether it would get any traction; we just wanted to put some positive energy out into the world.

Within two months, we cracked 100,000 fans and gained a 6 million person reach.

Fast forward nine months.

When we posted the below note to our Punnky Facebook page on September 16th, 2013, we had no idea what was coming next.

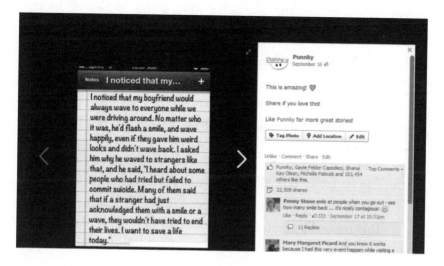

In the space of a few days, there were over 100,000 likes and 22,000 shares. How did it go so viral?

There are a few reasons:

1. Our Punnky fan page already had over 100,000 fans, so it was starting from a good base. Angela Yeow, who looks after the content for Punnky, has taken extremely good care of the fan base.

2. We've applied our online marketing skills and conversion rate optimisation techniques to this page (even though it's for a non-profit). For example, Angela tested sending fifteen different styles of content (e.g. regular text post, image, video etc.) and also different content themes (love, funny, relationships). Here's the results of Angela's analysis:

Row Labels	Posts	Total engage	Weighted engage	Average engage
CUTE PHOTO	5	11,971	15,543	3,109
FUNNY PHOTO	2	2,004	2,625	1,313
PHOTO STORY	10	13,963	19,209	1,921
COOL PHOTO	2	3,702	4,861	2,431
CARTOON/COMICS	3	9,238	13,981	4,660
SPECIAL OCCASSION GREETING	4	5,796	8,373	2,093
STORY	1	2,568	2,993	2,993
PUNNKY VIDEO	2	271	333	167
Grand Total	29	49,513	67,918	2,342

Row Labels	Posts	Total engage	Weighted engage	Average engage
Animals	5	15,726	21,220	4,244
Babies/Children	2	2,547	3,198	1,599
Inspiring others	7	12,698	18,826	2,689
Old couple love	1	1,534	1,827	1,827
Random act of kindness	2	636	778	389
Other	2	271	333	167
Special Occassion	7	11,919	16,744	2,392
Saving Lives	2	3,942	4,721	2,361
Promotion	1	240	271	271
Grand Total	29	49,513	67,918	

What we found was that images with a short caption work the best. We also tested what the description should be to get the best results. We found that a one-line description, followed by "Share if you <agree/love this/...>" and then "Like Punnky for more great stories" works the best. I'm not saying this is the perfect formula that will work for your fan page, but it works well for us.

3. The image is very different. It is a screenshot of the "notes" app from an iPhone and appears to be a personal message. This naturally creates curiosity—I wonder what this personal message is?

4. It satisfies Bret Gregory's theory on how to make a post go viral because of the integral effect.

In 2012, Professor Kathleen Milkman of Wharton University published a study in the *Journal of Marketing* where she and her colleagues studied over 7,000 *New York Times* posts and looked to see which ones would go most viral. They found that there was very strong correlation between content that was highly emotionally charged and the content that got shared the most. This is a concept known as "the integral effect."

In Professor Milkman's same study, she found that positive photos and content are much more likely to go viral than negative content. This quality is called "valence." Researchers in this study found that content that was more positive or had the most positive valence, as well as the most highly charged, emotionally-loaded content, was more likely to go viral.

This Punnky post satisfied the integral effect and also the positive valence test, which is why it went viral.

Using LinkedIn To Connect With Hard To Reach People

Affiliate partners and executives are tough to get in touch with. Cold calling is hard, even if you follow the tips I shared in Chapter 6. Sending cold emails is tough. Sending direct mail is expensive. A lot of people don't have fax machines anymore. How on earth are you meant to contact anyone these days?

A secret weapon a lot of people don't exploit is LinkedIn. You can think of LinkedIn as "social selling," where you sell without selling— if that makes sense!

It's so much easier to connect through LinkedIn than any other "cold" way of connecting.

As I was writing this book, I had to make contact with dozens of people to interview them and get their tips and permission to share their content for the book. For any new contact, I went exclusively through LinkedIn to connect. And the majority of people were happy to help.

Here's how I did it:

1. Made sure my profile was completely filled in, with lots of recommendations, endorsements, and social proof. Think about it from your target's perspective. When you get a connection request, the first thing you do is read the requestor's profile, right? So you want to make that profile look as professional and solid as possible!

2. I wrote a customised approach request for each person. Here's a short one that worked wonders:

Hi <firstname>

I'm writing a new best-selling book about creative marketing campaigns and I'd like to include some case studies from <company name> in there. Does this interest you?

Robert Coorey

3. Once I got connected with the person, I got in touch straight-away and shot for a Skype meeting as soon as possible. Get 'em while they're hot.

4. I then completed the interview and got my content.

This is exactly the same process you can follow whether you are trying to sell someone something, trying to get a partner on board as an affiliate or joint venture, or getting some advice from an expert.

Action Exercise: Pick ten people who would be awesome for you to meet and be connected with. Use the LinkedIn strategies above to connect and meet up with them.

How To Make Pinterest A Pillar Of Your Launch Strategy

Pinterest works wonders for most. For others, it might take a little more effort. But it's just a matter of degree.

Some businesses and individuals have an innate Pinterest advantage. Because Pinterest has an 80 percent female audience, some businesses are obvious Pinterest winners from the onset like those in fashion, travel, accessories, and design, since their activities lend themselves to being photographed beautifully. For these companies or individuals with an innate Pinterest advantage, the snowball effect has been remarkable.

For instance, here is a Pinterest winner: Better Homes and Gardens (BHG).

How A Home And Gardening Website Attracted 450,000 Followers On Pinterest

BHG knew it was a perfect fit for Pinterest right from the start—it knew its content was very pin-able even when the platform was on beta. In the beginning, the team tried to keep its Pinterest boards more niche, but it eventually found more success when it focused on broader themes. Currently, the Better Homes and Gardens brand on Pinterest has over 450,000 followers and more than 132 boards dedicated to gardening trends, quick and easy recipes, party ideas, home design and decor, and much more.

The Secret Software Tool To Identify The Most Viral Content To Share On Pinterest

Research has always been key for BHG's success, and it has always watched what people are pinning from its site using Curalate, identifying trends that it should be covering and constantly learning from its pins. BHG tracked pins, repinned, and paid special attention to organic pins (pins that originate from users vs. repinning their own pins, etc.).

Pinterest has played a crucial role in helping BHG understand its readers better, and it has allowed the BHG social media team to identify through Pinterest its ideal persona, someone who "is very DIY focused, loves the step by steps, is backing up a storm, and starts getting inspired for the holidays WAY earlier than we anticipated," explains BHG's Digital Editorial Manager Kaelin Zawilinski. Bloggers have also been subject to scrutiny by BHG—whatever a blogger pins is a potentially interesting topic and, therefore, a topic worth exploring.

Zawilinski also implemented a few other strategies that have taken the BHG team to serious Pinterest heights. Some of them are as simple as promoting a big banner on their own website encouraging readers to visit their Pinterest boards. Or having a teaser in every pin urging you to click on the link back to BHG's website. Here's an example of a great teaser:

"How to get curb appeal on a dime"—click on the caption and you are redirected to a wealth of fun and innovative suggestions to turn your old driveway into a colourful oasis. BHG designed the page in a format that is conversion friendly by presenting advertising space and ecommerce links.

The Zawilinski genius and her team have created numerous other campaigns, many very successful like the "Pin and Win Your Better Homes and Gardens Dream Home" challenge. Contestants created Dream Home Pinterest boards comprised of their favourite BHG images from BHG.com. The magazine's editors selected winning boards based on visual cohesiveness and creative descriptions. This campaign attracted over 11,400 Pinterest fans.

Another winning strategy was to collaborate with popular pinners who already had a large following. Working with pinner Jennifer Chong, for instance, became an extremely profitable partnership for BHG.

Jennifer pins content from BHG's website to the Pinterest-owned board, which exposes all of Jennifer's nearly two-and-a-half million followers to BHG's content and to the BHG Pinterest account. As Jennifer's audience follows the board, BHG's follower numbers grow.

How Sephora Generates More Revenue From Pinterest Than Facebook

Then there is Sephora (http://www.pinterest.com/sephora)

The beauty industry giant was made for Pinterest or Pinterest was made for Sephora. The order is irrelevant; what really is important here is the synergy between these two businesses. With over 200,000 followers and 5,000 pins, Sephora knows exactly what its beauty community wants. By using Pinterest Web Analytics to observe the kinds of content that get the most pins and repins, Sephora has come to learn which content will be popular with pinners—such as beauty lists, color swatches, and face charts.

Sephora's social media team first noticed Pinterest users were saving their favourite beauty products and inspirations on pinboards. Sephora didn't take long to reach out to them and start its own Pinterest crusade by adding a "Pin it" button to every product on its website.

Then it began a stunning campaign called "Sephora Color Wash," which aimed to help pinners get used to the newly revamped site and browse through Sephora's catalogs.

Next, Sephora personally addressed all pinners via email. That email was repinned 14,000 times—pretty uncommon at a time when most emails get deleted!—and it resulted in a 60 percent growth in traffic from Pinterest to Sephora's website.

Julie Borstein, CMO and Chief Digital Officer at Sephora, explains that "when we create content for their site or emails, we think of additional ways that we can help the story along on Pinterest. We use web analytics to look at top pins, test quote layouts from brand founders, and try different product shots—we spend time learning about what works and experiment often to get it right."

One particularly successful strategy was the use of boards to store "It Lists." "We get asked quite often which are our favorite products," continues Borstein. "We were eager to share our expertise, and encourage clients to save their own. But before Pinterest, there wasn't an easy or scalable place to share the story of our staff's 'It Lists.' So, the It Lists were created by Sephora staff to make it easy to highlight their own favourite products as well as any special product tips and tricks. Sephora clients can pin these products to their own lists as favourites or later purchases."

These lists help Sephora's clients to remember which products interest them, and they makes it easy for the clients to find those products when they are ready to shop. The It Lists have now become one of the company's most followed boards, and Sephora is looking to create even more ways to share lists to continue its popularity. Currently, its very qualified pinners tend to spend fifteen times more money on Sephora.com than the average Facebook fan.

The Secrets Of A 4.5M Follower Pinterest Powerhouse

Jetsetter knows it has been born with the Pinterest silver spoon, but it has always looked for very creative ways to engage with its online community and understand what type of content appealed to its customers.

Through its Jetsetter Curator promotion, for instance, the company invited over a million members to create boards reflecting the most inspiring travel destinations across four theme categories: escape, adventure, style, and cosmopolitan. A panel of celebrity judges, including Arianna Huffington and the editor-in-chief of *Harper's Bazaar*, Glenda Bailey, selected winning boards where the best pinners earned a prize.

Fans pinned over 50,000 images in less than a month. Pinterest referral traffic increased 100 percent, and Jetsetter page views increased by 150 percent.

"When we unleashed our community to share their favorite Jetsetter content on Pinterest," explains Jon Goldman, Jetsetter's Social Media Manager, "it generated a ton of ideas for how to make our own Pinterest boards more compelling. We also learned which photos on our site resonate the most with our users and it's since influenced our content strategy."

Jetsetter also launched an online scavenger hunt called "Pin Your Way to Paradise."

Members were prompted with daily clues over a two-week period and challenged to pin photos that best matched each of the clues. In response, Jetsetter's community created over 800 boards and 16,000 pins—judged on their visual interest, creativity, and originality, and how well they matched the daily clues.

In addition to offering inspirational travel content, Jetsetter wanted to prove the fun behind planning an incredible trip, so it collaborated with a passionate Jetsetter fan to plan the fan's vacation to Turks & Caicos. Together, they pinned ideas for everyone else to see—what to bring, what to wear, what to do, where to go, what to eat—always showing the versatility and interactivity of Jetsetter's site.

The Turks & Caicos Board reached over 720,000 Pinterest followers, and engaged users pinned more than 9,500 times.

How A Pet Insurer Gets Leads From Pinterest

Veterinary Pet Insurer Petplan also saw in Pinterest the perfect tool for the purpose of visually showcasing its expertise and conveying its brand personality.

Starting from its clever use of funny board titles—like "Cat-astrophes averted" or "Pawsitively cute pets" or "We wear this"—that just make you want to click immediately to the company's educational content boards for pet health or boards expanding into specifics such as breeding and health tips...Petplan's extremely smart use of Pinterest has led to increased 69 percent more page views and 97 percent greater time-on-site than Twitter.

Petplan also consolidated its Pinterest approach by adding "Pin It" buttons and links in emails, social campaigns, and its website products. As soon as that happened, it saw an 87 percent increase in new site traffic, a 35 percent increase in page views and a 12.5 percent increase in insurance quote requests. Not bad for a pet insurer.

How An Infographic Got 30,000 Pins On Pinterest And 6,000 Website Visits

Infographics are worth exploring, even in a female-dominated platform like Pinterest. Ask Andreaa Ayers, whose infographic received 30,000 pins on Pinterest. This is what he did....

After creating the infographic, he immediately created a blog post about the infographic and urged others to share it on their blogs. He then shared the infographic on Pinterest on a board titled "Marketing Tips" and encouraged his Pinterest followers to share it as well. At that time, he had about 2,500 followers to that board. He then went on to send links to the blog post to his list of contacts and shared it on social media (Twitter, Facebook, LinkedIn, Google+, etc.). A day later, he had over 400 people who re-pinned it on Pinterest and over 600 new visitors to his website.

It gets better. A few days later, he reached out to some top bloggers and websites, and by the next Sunday, the infographic was shared over 1,000 times on Pinterest. He received over 11,000 page views and over 6,000 visits to his website. Lucky Andreaa was then picked up by influential marketing bloggers like Denise Wakeman and popular sites like Ragan.com, who shared it with their readers. This resulted in even more traffic to his site, more repins, and more newsletter subscribers. And so on and so forth until Andreaa hit 30,000 pins.

But what about those who lack the visual appeal or whose stories are not as inspirational or easy to relate to?

Is there doom for them in the Pinterest universe?

Not necessarily.

How wikiHow Went From 0 To 46,000 Pinterest Followers In A Few Months

Pinterest has worked very well for the world's How-to-Manual, wiki-How, which managed to turn the dullness generally associated with instructions and step-by-step guides into a vast visual journey dotted with humour and fun for Pinterest users.

Thom Scher, Director of Marketing at wikiHow, explains that in a short period of time, wikiHow managed to go from 0 to 46,000 followers, and initially, without giving it much thought—just posting ad-hoc content, without investing too much effort. But somehow, organically, it generated a few thousand followers. So when it realized Pinterest was generating a significant amount of engagement and referrals from a very minimal following, Thom decided to invest some serious time with the network, redeveloping the original boards and focusing on Pinterest-popular topics, pinning only things that had higher quality visuals, and watching what topic areas did well.

And then, on to cross-promotion—links (and announcements) were added to wikiHow's other social media sites, its newsletter frequently pushed Pinterest-related content, and its homepage for wikiHow.com received a banner five-plus days a week that advertised for people to follow it on Pinterest.

That was it. Numbers began to grow exponentially.

As of today, wikiHow has nearly reached 50,000 followers.

"Cross-promotion and harnessing of other social networks and traffic, once our Pinterest page was better equipped to showcase the wikiHow brand," was the key, emphasizes Thom. But other strategies were also very successful, like promoting the content in the more popular categories and popular topics. Seasonal items (holidays, back to school, summer) consistently generated traction too so they were also encouraged. For instance:

How to Take a Detox Bath: Perfect for Pinterest's female demographic.

How to Read Palms: A fun topic that successfully feeds people's curiosity.

How to Clean a Toilet with Coke: Humorous, entertaining images that made it a winner with Pinterest audiences.

How to Get Rid of Blackheads: High quality content for the perfect demographic.

Then it was time to get the popular pinners on their side. Thom and his team contacted some top pinners, and after improving articles on their site that they believed would do particularly well on Pinterest, they added the Pin-It button site-wide to get more articles into the general Pinterest feed. When someone arrives at wikiHow via Pinterest, more Pinterest-prime content is presented to the customer, keeping the engagement on some of wikiHow's top pins alive and fresh.

Three factors are core to wikiHow's success, according to Scher:

1. Visually appealing posts

2. Topics that fit in with the demographic of the audience

3. High-quality click-through material

How Kotex Got 694,853 Interactions By Running The First Ever Pinterest Contest

Kotex is also working hard to create engaging Pinterest strategies to help it present a fresh, youthful image for the twenty-first-century woman.

Again, perfect demographic, and a clever team that has used the inherent femininity in these usually hard-to-market hygiene products to its advantage. How?

Kotex came up with the first Pinterest campaign in the world and called it "Inspiration Day." After locating fifty influential female users of Pinterest, Kotex found out what motivated and inspired these women, and it posted virtual gifts (images) based on these users' pins and interests. Not only that, these ladies were also rewarded in real life by having the actual gift delivered to their homes if they re-pinned the virtual gifts.

And re-pin they did!

Almost 100 percent of the women re-pinned and talked about their gifts and went on posting comments on Facebook and on Twitter and even on Instagram.

The final result? A total of 2,284 interactions on Pinterest and 694,853 interactions across all sites.

The lesson? Touch the heart of those who have a say and you will be rewarded by the Pinterest snowball effect.

Action Exercise: Get your Pinterest page online right away. Use the strategies in this chapter that are the most suited to your business, whether it's a competition, reaching out to Pinterest influencers, or cross-promoting with your other channels.

Reddit—A Gem Of A Social Network!

Not everyone gets Reddit.

To be honest, this social news and entertainment website can be a little intimidating and disorienting. The average user of Reddit is the young, male, sceptical, liberal, geeky, Internet-literate, and ever-so-meta audience who participates on this giant bulletin board.

Plus, you know what? I'm just going to say it out loud and be prepared for the consequences—I don't like ugly sites. I much prefer good-looking sites, and Reddit just cut it! I personally need to relate to a website's aesthetic proposition. Yes, I know; how very superficial of me. And I bet if I were to dare to make this comment on Reddit itself, I'd probably be eaten alive.

Thankfully for Reddit's creators, Alexis Ohanian and Steve Huffman, more than 28 million monthly users just in the U.S. are a lot savvier than me and look for more than just appealing pictures and sliders (but just to stop digging this hole even deeper for myself, let me clarify that I think poor content sucks, and we should rid the Internet of it—but I also feel that if good content is accompanied by pleasant imagery, all the better). You've got to admit, there is a clunkiness to Reddit's user interface. In fact, it has barely been updated since these two college grads started in 2005. And yet, Reddit attracts 3.4 billion page views a month, a figure that places it among the seventy most visited sites in the U.S.

Reddit features over 185,000 forums where users can have their say on anything from science trivia, to videogame reviews, political debates, jokes, and endless amounts of photos, most of them of cats or naked women. Yes, naked women.

Reddit is not precisely the kind of platform that attracts elegant fashion houses or sports car advertisers. But under Snoo's watchful eye (Reddit's goofy red-eyed alien logo), there is a super-engaged audience that discusses and votes on content that other users have submitted.

In the case of Neil Degrasse Tyson, author, radio host, TV host, planetarium director, and a big thinker on life and the universe, Reddit has paved the path for his instant success with his recent AMA session ("Ask Me Anything," a series of threads that run like online Q&A sessions). Neil conducted a session designed to answer the Internet's most pressing questions about *Cosmos: A Space-Time Odyssey*, which airs in 2014 on the Fox channel. His AMA session received 10,634 comments, double the number of comments of the top scoring AMA post of all time by longtime Jeopardy winner Ken Jennings. How good would it be if you could receive over 10,000 comments?

How Are The Big Guys Using Reddit?

The big guys know they can't shout their message on Reddit. They need to interact with their very curious audience, which is ever-so-willing to learn. Once they capture the audience's attention, their efforts on Reddit tend to translate directly into huge sales increases. So marketers are not leaving anything to chance when it comes to Reddit; they are actually hanging out, chatting with their audiences. Real people doing real things.

Really?

Ryan Holiday, the bestselling author of *Trust Me, I'm Lying: Confessions of a Media Manipulator*, is sceptical about the brands' apparent good-will. After all, Ryan explains, the best kind of marketing messages are the ones that don't seem like marketing messages because the defences of target audiences are down and are then easy to capture. In the last year, some of the big players have made conspicuous appearances on Reddit in what at first glance appeared to be organic and genuine discussions by Reddit users, but they ended up being some serious marketing being put to work.

It may be possible that some of these positive messages have been posted by legitimate users and fans. Or they could very well have been posted directly by the self-promoting brands themselves, or perhaps given an extra push by paid promotion. Ryan goes as far as claiming that what's going on Reddit these days has media manipulation written all over it. Harmless, if you will, like brand messaging passing as content, but manipulation. It's hard to say until someone is caught blatantly violating the rules and ends up receiving an embarrassing "Hail Corporate" tag.

Deception or not, many marketers are dying to incorporate Reddit in their marketing mix.

Why? Simple.

Many other big businesses had a chance to feel the Redditors' love. Love translates into serious cash and, ultimately, that's what matters.

How To Get To The Front Page Of Reddit

Costco is one such case. The retailer made it to Reddit's front page multiple times via the "Today I Learned" (TIL) subreddit, amassing more than 40,000 "upvotes" (an "upvote" is comparable to a "Like" on Facebook) and over 3,000 comments, most of them about how awesome Costco is. The "Hot dog and soda combo for $1.50 not changing for 21 years" Reddit received 3,100 upvotes and 2,400 comments.

The company's honourable business practices were also hailed by many, with 2,700 upvotes and 1,100 comments. Is there anything better for a company than to get people commenting on its outstanding customer services and having its own employees affirm how much they enjoy working for it?

Volvo went along with a similar strategy to Costco's. With a post on the "Today I Learned" subreddit honouring Volvo for giving free license on the three-point seat belt, the comment section soon became a brand booster for Volvo as well as a mutilator against Apple for its reputation for suing over patents. The TIL post resulted in the fifth highest link in the TIL subreddit with 5,400 upvotes and 1,300 comments.

But Costco and Volvo are not the only ones getting the Reddit love.

How Do You Get Reddit Traffic If You Don't Bother To Be Active On The Network?

To gain traffic, Pennsylvania-based search engine company **Duck Duck Go** went the old fashioned way and placed an ad on Reddit. The result, though, far exceeded earlier marketing attempts. The simple ad ran for thirteen days, cost $650 in total, yielding 20,700 clicks. The Reddit ads proved to be much more successful than the ads the company placed on other platforms like AdWords, Yahoo, Bing, Facebook, MySpace, and StumbleUpon.

Apart from the incredible cost-per-click of 3.14 cents, the company received a lot of feedback in the form of comments, which were very helpful for developers to fix bugs and implement new features.

Gabriel Weinberg, Duck Duck Go founder, thinks it is the nature of curious Redditors that works. "They actually try out your site. 3 cents per unique visitor is pretty good in and of itself, but it's all worthless unless they actually try out your site. For example, you can get 5c unique visitors from StumbleUpon (presumably in a similar demographic), but StumbleUpon visitors never would try out my sites. Reddit visitors did try out Duck Duck Go." Plus Redditors have the option to comment on ads. In his case, Gabriel received 656 comments! The comments thread is immensely useful because it helps you learn and go back to the drawing board, fix bugs, implement new feature requests, and learn about first impressions.

Getting 500 Training Course Signups On Reddit

And then you have the case of the **Udemy Hebrew course**.

When Hebrew instructor Bogdan Milanovich posted on Reddit about his Udemy course, he had no idea the kind of beast he was unleashing.

Jewish customers presenting the Reddit coupon were able to join the course for free. Well, in under two days, 500 people enrolled in his course. Yes, for free, but wait—this strategy caused a ripple effect of paid signups. Here's why:

Bogdan took the opportunity to market cleverly to a new community who under other circumstances wouldn't have paid for his course anyway. So, in a way, he was not really butchering his own paid sales or losing out on income. Besides, because courses with more students convert at higher rates than courses with less students, the more students he enrolled in the course, the bigger his credibility boost.

Now Bogdan can cross sell the 500 free students and have them become paid students for future courses he publishes. If the students like Bogdan's first course, then chances are they will be willing to pay for the next course(s) he publishes.

When Someone Complains On Reddit, You Profit!

Talking about taking opportunities.

BridgfordStore Beef Jerky noticed a discussion on Reddit complaining about the high cost of beef jerky. It took full advantage of the situation by promoting its own product through a unique discount code, exclusive to Reddit users, for beef jerky.

The result?

Tons of sales and hundreds of loyal fans who then were eager to find out more about sales-related statistics regarding the discount. A truly curious lot, those Redditors; that's for sure.

So, What Sends Submissions On Reddit To Stardom?

It's all about the title.

Yep, you are probably thinking, "Thanks for that; great discovery, Rob."

But let me just repeat the obvious. If you haven't worked it out by now…the Reddit audience is savvy, switched on, and extremely aggressive if you do the wrong thing by it! I heard Alexis in an interview say once, "You wouldn't just walk up to a group of people at a party and say, 'Hey, buy my stuff.'" You'd start by introducing yourself and getting to know the people first.

In saying that, I'm not personally bothered myself to get on there and engage heavily. But there are a lot of community managers who love doing this! Like with Facebook, Twitter, and the others, you can appoint a community manager to handle this for you by getting in there and talking to the user base. And that's a great thing. When you combine this with paid ads (at 3c a click, you almost can't go wrong, right?), Reddit is certainly a channel you would be wise to play in.

Action Exercise: Get onto Reddit. Set up an account. If you like engaging in social media, by all means, get engaged. Otherwise, open up an advertising account and test a small ad budget to your landing page. Check the difference in cost-per-click and conversion rate compared to your other traffic sources.

Dell Earns $6.5 Million, Thanks To Twitter

Those who say Twitter is nothing more than a place where people share inconsequential experiences in their lives might want to listen up. Dell told Bloomberg News that it has earned an estimated $6.5 million in sales of PCs, accessories, and software, thanks to promotions on Twitter. Dell's Twitter accounts are followed by people in twelve countries. Brazil users alone spent $800,000 in an eight-month period.

How Did Dell Do It?

Dell joins companies like Starbucks, JetBlue, and Whole Foods as one of the most active corporate Twitter users. "It's a great way to fix customer problems and hear what customers have to say, it's a great feedback forum and it leads to sales—how can you miss?" said Richard Binhammer, who worked in Dell's corporate affairs office and was active on Dell's Twitter accounts.

Dell uses Twitter to send out coupons, including some that are exclusive to its Twitter followers. It is particularly useful for the Dell Outlet because the inventory of returned and refurbished products fluctuates. If the outlet gets thirty flat-screen televisions one week, for example, it can alert its customers.

Dell also announces company and product news and talks directly with customers, responding to complaints or asking for feedback. There are about 200 Dell employees who talk to customers on Dell's Twitter accounts, from a gaming expert to a server expert to members of the chief technology officer's staff.

Action Exercise: How can you use Twitter to share great deals or clear excess inventory?

SlideShare And StumbleUpon—Two Hidden Gems

Now, we have **SlideShare**—the sleeping giant of digital marketing.

Acquired by LinkedIn in March 2012, SlideShare is a convenient slide compilation and distribution platform designed to inspire and persuade audiences that might be tempted to focus their attention elsewhere.

Some quick stats: With over 50 million unique visitors a month, SlideShare is one of the top 150 sites on the web.

SlideShare visitors actually do spend a considerable amount of time sifting through additional content, rather than bouncing after their initial visit, as is usual with the majority of sites. There are over 1,100 slides being studied at any given moment—a really significant level of viewership in online marketing.

Most of the presentations you'll find on SlideShare are extremely useful for visitors conducting research at work, the majority of this platform's audience. So, if you are using the website and its services as a strategic marketing tool, you can make it a substantial weapon in your lead generation arsenal.

Surprised? I know, you probably didn't realise SlideShare was, in fact, a marketing tool. Indeed, it is a lot more than a mere glorified PowerPoint. For businesses using this platform, the potential behind SlideShare is immense.

Jake Wengroff of business growth specialist firm Frost & Sullivan has tasted the SlideShare potential himself. Jake says SlideShare makes it easy to take the assets you already have as a business owner to a much wider audience, resulting in thousands of qualified leads a year, and a fifty times return on investment.

And—in stark contrast to most business' experiences with social media today—it delivers measurement based on real business activity, like leads.

Popular blogger, podcaster, and best-selling author Mitch Joel is a renowned thought leader in the new media space. Mitch runs Twist Image, a fast-growing digital marketing agency in Canada, and takes his knowledge on strategic thinking and his technical expertise to various conferences throughout the world.

But even someone as experienced as Joel was pleasantly surprised when "25+ Mind Blowing Stats About Business Today," a presentation he created to promote his new book *CTRL ALT Delete*, quickly surged to 45,000+ views on SlideShare.

Today, that number has jumped to over 135,000. By contrast, a YouTube video featuring the same statistics—but produced by a third party, not Joel—had received just over 1,000 views.

Joel attributes the success of his presentation on SlideShare to its being informative and entertaining in a way that not only solved a serious problem a lot of businesses have once they get into a state of stagnation, but it did so interestingly.

Just as text-heavy PowerPoint presentations put everyone to sleep in boardrooms or conferences, similarly, they're not excessively popular on SlideShare. Take your audience on a visual journey—that's Mitch's advice.

Renowned author Seth Godin is another expert SlideSharer who agrees with Joel: Your slides have to reinforce your words, not repeat them. You need to create slides that demonstrate, with emotional proof, that what you're saying is true, not just accurate.

So make sure your slide triggers an emotional reaction in the audience. You want viewers to sit up and want to know what you're going to say that fits in with that image, explains Godin. Then, if you do it right, every time they think of what you said, they'll see the image (and vice versa). If you are talking about pollution in Houston, for instance, "instead of giving me four bullet points of EPA data, why not read me the stats but show me a photo of a bunch of dead birds, some smog and even a diseased lung? This is cheating! It's unfair! It works."

Unfair advantage from the hand of a quiet Internet giant—SlideShare.

Why not?

While everyone else is still unaware of SlideShare's potential, you can go for it and use the surprise element to your advantage. Later in this chapter, you'll see how to drive a bucket-load of cheap traffic to your SlideShare.

And to help achieve ultimate content in your slides, make sure you bring another quiet giant of digital marketing onboard: StumbleUpon.

StumbleUpon is one of the top sources of social media traffic in the U.S.

Stunned?

Good.

Because StumbleUpon can drive some solid traffic to your site producing some really unexpected results.

According to Shell Harris, TopTenz' creator, StumbleUpon basically built his website. His "Top ten civilisations that mysteriously disappeared" received nearly 700,000 stumbles. That's some serious traffic that can result in a pretty lucrative income stream.

But how?

Or even better, let's start right from the start: What is StumbleUpon?

StumbleUpon is your digital content butler, if you want. It's the site you trust to deliver the hot topics that matter to you. Since its inception in 2001, StumbleUpon has been serving new and interesting content from across the Web to over 25 million subscribers. In addition, more than 80,000 brands, publishers, and other marketers have used StumbleUpon's Paid Discovery platform to tell their stories and promote their products and services.

What Does StumbleUpon Mean For You?

It means high traffic volumes.

It means leaving very clear signposts for readers to stumble upon, selectively creating a connection with the kind of audience that really matters to your business.

Some people might say you should take StumbleUpon traffic with a grain of salt. Yes, that might be right, but don't completely discount it as insignificant. In many cases, a brand's longtime stumblers and advocates have contributed to make its content go viral in very effective ways.

Once a person becomes a Stumbler, the engine will deliver articles, images, videos, and other forms of content based upon the person's profile and interests.

How A New York City Startup Got 6,000 Signups In One Week Through StumbleUpon...With Just $77 In Advertising Spend

A few years ago, Alex Mitchell, an independent musician, discovered how difficult it was to be discovered in New York City. Out of this frustration, Alex and a couple of friends built hypetree in 2011, a tool that compares the music of two different independent bands, prompting the music fan to choose the tune that strikes his fancy more. Alex and his friends had an awesome product; now they were stuck with an issue: How would indie music fans discover their service?

To start with, they wanted to get about 1,000 sign-ups for a beta version of their product. They resorted to StumbleUpon.

Mitchell started a paid StumbleUpon campaign, with a huge budget of $77 (yes, just $77).

And that was a good move. Stumblers loved hypetree's campaign, which averaged about a 90 percent positive rating, generating 182,000 free stumbles and over 1,700 paid stumbles.

"Our StumbleUpon campaign worked so overwhelmingly well that we exceeded our month goal within the first day," explains Mitchell in an interview by Jack Krawczyk. "Our campaign was designed to spread awareness of our product across several ad platforms in an attempt to get at least 1,000 people to sign up for our beta in the first month."

They got six times that number of subscribers in one week. The traffic crashed hypetree's servers.

According to Michelle Panzironi, head of Operations & Marketing for hypetree, "StumbleUpon is not just about getting clicks, it's about winning the user over with your content."

How A Social Network For Families "Crushed It" On StumbleUpon

The team behind HatchedIt, the social network for families, had exactly this objective in mind—to attract busy parents to the site and help them coordinate their busy family schedules. Obviously, they had to spread the word to achieve their objectives. StumbleUpon, Google, and Facebook composed the marketing budget for the HatchedIt team.

For a period of two weeks, HatchedIt allocated 40 percent of its budget to StumbleUpon, 40 percent to Google, and 20 percent to Facebook. With each service, the team looked to target a demographic of women who were age thirty-plus, seeking to entice moms or soon-to-be moms. By the end of that two-week period, StumbleUpon had driven nearly twice as many conversions as the other two platforms combined.

Kirsten Bischoff, one of the HatchedIt cofounders, explains that she attributes much of their success with this platform to the fact that "StumbleUpon's users are reaching our site while in 'discovery mode'.... We are not only targeting people who are hoping to find new sites—but even better for us, people who are hoping to find new sites that are focused on family and parenting."

How A Freelance "One-Man Band" Designer Got 250,000 StumbleUpon Hits In One Year

Artists and designers, such as Aled Lewis, have also learnt to drive highly targeted audiences to their sites, reaching a much broader audience than would otherwise have been possible without the help of StumbleUpon. His website, aledlewis.com, received almost a quarter of a million hits in one year alone—and those are just the hits that StumbleUpon is responsible for. If you take into account the way people share links with their friends and loved ones, the actual number of hits that can be attributed to StumbleUpon rises even more.

So, should you neglect this gentle giant simply because it sits quietly under the shade of the giants of digital marketing?

No, you probably shouldn't unless your business activity is very localised. In that case, it will probably not work that well for you.

But if you are hoping to capture a much broader audience, don't wait. Give StumbleUpon a go, start running some ads, and then sit and wait. Be patient; the sleepy giant might just take its sweet while to deliver what you are after, but it'll get there.

Using StumbleUpon To Get On The Front Page Of Slideshare

Remember, before I said you will find out how to get cheap traffic to your SlideShare? Well, here it is:

Probably the best example of using StumbleUpon and SlideShare in tandem is Tim Ferriss. Ferriss' marketing agency Mekanism wanted to see whether it was possible to get some PowerPoint slides outlining the benefits of *The 4-Hour Chef* on the homepage of SlideShare. Mekanism would accomplish this by having the book rank on SlideShare's "Top Presentations of the Day" section.

First, a SlideShare deck was created to outline the benefits/chapters of *The 4-Hour Chef.* Next, the math was done to determine how many views, and in what period of time, were needed to drive the slides into the "Top Presentations of the Day" section. Based on Mekanism's observations, it seemed as though 15,000 views within a twenty-four-hour period was likely enough.

Having this understanding of required viewing density, Mekanism uploaded the slides to SlideShare, promoted the slides via paid StumbleUpon ads and drove the content to the homepage of SlideShare via "stumbles," ensuring that everyone who visited Slideshare's homepage the day of the launch would see the presentation. Brilliant!

Action Exercise: Get your slides onto SlideShare. If you have the time, engage on StumbleUpon and stumble on sites similar to yours. If you have the money, try a small paid campaign on StumbleUpon to send traffic to your SlideShare.

BONUS TIP:
A FAST WAY TO GAIN COMPETITIVE INTELLIGENCE

There are software tools out there that show you all of the advertising that your competitors are running, what websites the ads are placed on and how long they've been running for. Visit the free book resources section for my latest recommendations: http://www.feedastarvingcrowd.com/resources

8

RUNNING LOW-BUDGET, HIGH-RETURN YOUTUBE AND FACEBOOK CAMPAIGNS

"There is a profound and enduring beauty in simplicity, in clarity, in efficiency. True simplicity is derived from so much more than just the absence of clutter and ornamentation. It's about bringing order to complexity."
— Jony Ive

Jony Ive said these captivating words at the official launch video of the Apple IOS7.

If you didn't know they were the words of Apple's senior vice president, you would think they were written by a poet.

For me, Jony highlights an undeniable fact: Apple is redefining a lot more than just the way we work and the way our tools look. Apple is teaching us a new vocabulary, a new style of communicating with our customers, an uncluttered way of brand messaging. Apple communicates innovation in a simple and yet beautiful, almost poetic way.

The thing is, innovation, an essential element in the advancement of most businesses today, is not easy to communicate. Plus, you and I don't have the financial resources to develop and promote innovation as effectively as Apple does.

Forbes estimated that in 2010 alone at least 250,000 new products were launched globally. What's more, a recent study by IBM Global business showed that in an effort to create sustainable growth, 42 percent of CEOs were launching products and services, and 28 percent were launching new business models.

A new product is great, but a new product requires a successful launch.

Again, the Apple iPad launch is the poster child for successful launches today: 300,000 sold on the first day, 3 million in the first eighty days, and after sixteen months, a market share estimated at 70 percent, despite a myriad of competitors.

But you and I don't have the resources, the tools, or the superb products that the geniuses at Apple have.

Instead, what we have to do is use the many platforms available to us today and apply all our wit and creativity to attract the interest of the type of quality customers we are after.

YouTube and Facebook are the platforms to start with.

Note: You can head to the free book resources section (http://www.feedastarvingcrowd.com/resources) to get the links for many of the campaigns in this chapter.

How A "Homemade" YouTube Video Sold 2.3 Million Toothbrushes

Super low-budget online videos have worked extremely well for Orabrush, a small Utah-based company. Bob Wagstaff, Ph.D., invented the Orabrush while supervising a team of Mormon missionaries in the Philippines. Apparently, Dr. Wagstaff, an engineer, was receiving complaints from the locals that his young missionaries had terrible breath. He decided to use the brush he had previously designed to clean chicken skins for a client and apply it to the human tongue, which is very similar to bumpy chicken skin.

Although the brush worked well, Wagstaff was having a tough time convincing consumers to buy a product they didn't know they needed. After eight years of trying to sell Orabrush to drug stores and retail chains, he was ready to give up. But then in 2009, he challenged marketing students at the Marriott School of Management at Brigham Young University to figure out how to sell the brushes online.

Unfortunately, the research conducted by the students revealed that 92 percent of people surveyed said that while they would try the tongue-cleaner, they were unlikely to buy it online. Another BYU student, Jeff Harmon, now chief marketing officer for Orabrush, heard about the project. He encouraged Wagstaff to try to reach the 8 percent who might buy the $4.49 brush online. Craig created a very low-budget movie featuring himself as the main actor, dressed in a lab coat and giant plastic goggles, who enthusiastically demonstrated in a series of online videos how cleaning your tongue can prevent bad breath.

The clips were so popular that sales continue to soar today. Orabrush has sold about 2.3 million brushes and has 313,000 Facebook fans. And based on the success of its viral video campaign, Orabrush now has distribution through major retailers, including CVS and Wal-Mart.

How Blending Weird Stuff On Camera Got 100 Million Views And Bumped Sales By 700 Percent

The Blendtec "Will it Blend?" series of viral videos started when then-new marketing director, George Wright, found out that CEO

Tom Dickson and the research team had a practice of blending up wooden boards to test the product toughness. Wright then thought, "Why not shoot a video of the operation and post it online?" With a $100 budget, he invested in supplies and convinced Dickson to blend up other things on camera.

186 videos later, Blendtec's retail sales are up a reported 700 percent, its YouTube site has 200,000+ subscribers, and it has been featured on major mainstream media outlets like *The Today Show*, *The Tonight Show*, The History Channel, *The Wall Street Journal*, and others. Overall, the "Will It Blend?" series has accumulated more than 100,000,000 hits, and it doesn't look like it's going to slow down any time soon.

They just had a blender, a video camera or iPhone, and a lab coat. That's all.

How A $5,000 Budget Got Over 4 Million Views And 12,000 Sales

Michael Dubin, the star of the Dollar Shave Club video and founder of Los Angeles-based Dollar Shave Club, didn't do too bad a job trying. From a machete-wielding CEO to a shaving baby to a goofy dance number, the tightly scripted video, "Our Blades Are F**king Great," caught everyone's attention, entertaining people and making them laugh.

Michael and his team succeeded at telling a story through a visual narrative with the brand/product as a thread in the talking point. They kept it top level and focused on entertaining the viewer. What did everyone take away from that video? That Dollar Shave Club's blades are "F***ing Great."

Forty-eight hours after the video debuted on YouTube, and $5,000 later, some 12,000 people signed up for the service. Besides some Google ads, the business had not invested in any other form of marketing. Three months after the video's great debut, it had racked up 4.75 million views—thanks in large part to shares on social media sites. Today, over 11 million people have watched Michael and his team. "Our blades are f**king great" has been the company's unofficial slogan ever since.

But let's talk even lower budget. As low as it can probably get.

How An Australian Gardener Scored 160,000 Views With An Egg And A Plastic Bottle

In this case, you just need an egg and a plastic bottle.

That's how Brisbane gardener Greg Hadley has been captivating millions of people—a big fat smile, a cheeky Aussie accent, and an egg.

Greg is the creator of several channels, including Greg the Gardener and Greg's Kitchen. Since his first video launch two years ago, "Welcome to Greg the Gardener," he has been making thousands of dollars a month teaching people how to do everything from remove a tree stump (almost 160,000 views) to cooking simple lamb chops (more than 35,000 views). He also earns up to $12 for every thousand YouTube views through advertising revenue, a welcomed side income given he is getting over 8,000 views a day.

How A Fitness Trainer Turned YouTube Ads Into Cash

YouTube traffic is extremely cheap. At E-Web Marketing, we've done campaigns where the cost-per-view has been one cent. The biggest challenge is getting that traffic to convert. Mike Chang has cracked that code.

Who is Mike Chang? He's just an ordinary guy who shot a few workout videos and posted them to YouTube. Well, that's a bit of an understatement. Mike runs the #1 fitness channel on YouTube, with 1.9 million subscribers and over 240 million views.

Mike Chang's first appearance on YouTube cost him around $220.

Well that, and years of perfecting a technique to achieve perfectly chiseled abs. After creating Sixpackshortcuts.com, Chang began recording his workout routines and sharing them on a YouTube brand channel in October 2010. Today, Mike is the number one viewed YouTube trainer.

Five months after his first video, Mike uploaded one of his most popular videos, a 3.5-minute workout, the "Home Chest & Back Workout," which has had nearly 9 million views to date.

Most of Mike's sales leads today come through social media and YouTube, where potential customers can watch and try his workout system. He has taken the fitness information marketing industry by storm, so now we're going to analyse his sales funnel to see how he does it!

Mike starts with running YouTube ads in the top right-hand corner of the "suggested videos" section.

Once you click on Mike's ad, you'll go to his YouTube video page. A lot of Mike's videos are "piece to camera" where he speaks to the camera directly, but I've noticed a recent video where he is using a Jon Benson Whiteboard Video Sales letter—judging by the number of views (over 5 million)—you can safely assume this is doing quite well for him.

So once you watch the video, there is the overlay banner at the bottom of the video, and also the link in the video description box, both pointing you back to the sales page for the course.

You hit the sales page, click "order now," and just when you think you've finished by submitting your credit card details...instead of getting a thank you page with a receipt, you actually go to an upsell page, a course on how to get more muscle mass.

And then when you choose "Yes" or "No" to this upsell, you get hit with another upsell, which is a course to help you lose weight!

One of Mike's tactics is to auto-enroll customers in his advanced coaching program for a fourteen-day free trial. If you don't cancel within the trial period, you are charged $97/month for five months for the coaching.

This is where a big question mark comes up for me. It's known in the industry as "forced continuity," and is a popular way to turn one-time revenue into recurring income. Look, here's where things could go wrong for you if you force continuity....

What if people just want to buy the one time offer without the monthly continuity? When I see a monthly continuity, the first question that comes up in my mind is: "Oh man, it's going to be a real hassle to cancel this if I don't like it," and many other people have this same concern.

I'm not saying that Mike makes it hard to cancel. In fact, his customer service is very good. What I'm getting at is that this tactic could negatively affect his conversions. The question is: Would it affect conversions more than the extra revenue he gets from the upsell? I'm assuming Mike has tested and determined that it's worth it to have lower conversions but a higher customer lifetime value.

I would prefer to see a checkbox where you can opt-in for the free fourteen-day trial rather than forcing people into it, but that's just my preference.

Mike is doing really well online. Some of his sales language techniques are quite strong, so they might not suit your style of selling. Some of his sales pages might not look that pretty. But one thing you know for sure, they are converting.

You could do a lot worse than take a careful look at the sales funnel for Mike and emulate it for your business.

How A Fashion Brand Scored 7.5M Views, 1m Facebook Likes, And A 50% Sales Increase Using A Facebook Competition

In his outstanding book *Contagious: Why Things Catch On*, Jonah Berger explains the case of the iconic British brand Burberry. Feeling the pressure of the economic downturn, the iconic fashion house came up with "The Art of the Trench" campaign. Burberry encouraged its customers to tell the company's story by submitting photos of themselves wearing Burberry coats. The Burberry team wanted to give existing customers their "fifteen minutes of fame" as models on the site, and allow other customers to admire their sense of style. In the year following the launch of the Art of the Trench, Burberry's Facebook fan base grew to more than one million, the largest fan count in the luxury sector at the time. Ecommerce sales grew 50 percent year-over-year, and the site had 7.5 million views from 150 countries in the first year. Conversion rates from the Art of the Trench click-throughs to the Burberry website were significantly higher than those from other sources.

Those whose pictures were selected to run on the Burberry website became eager storytellers and evangelists themselves. Burberry found a way to have its own voice translated into the language of Facebook users, and in that way, it was able to make itself heard.

How A Travel Company Got 8,000 Fans And 10m Impressions Running A Facebook Competition

Contiki Vacations' Get On The Bus Facebook promotion also appealed to the need of Facebook users to have their stories broadcast and shared. Contiki was looking to generate awareness and purchase intent during the critical travel-booking season. To reach its younger target audience and capture the vibrant personality of the Contiki brand, Contiki developed "Get On The Bus," a fun and engaging contest application that ran within Contiki's Facebook Page. This clever strategy encouraged fans of Contiki to create their own virtual tour bus (complete with their own bus name and "story"), choose their trip, and invite and fill up their bus with four of their Facebook friends. Contestants had to campaign for votes for a chance to win the trip for the entire group, which was worth up to $25,000.

The Facebook page exclusively dedicated by Contiki to this competition provided a high level of personalisation and added an exciting game-like element to the program. Apart from showing the average age and gender of the passengers on the bus, each bus' "personality" was displayed through an interactive experience that incorporated the music, movies, Likes, and interests that passengers had in common via their Facebook profiles. Bus pages also included Facebook comments for bus-mates to communicate and strategise during the voting period, as well as Like buttons and sharing tools to get the word out about the promotion across their social graphs.

The result of this incredible well-orchestrated campaign was an increase of over 8,000 fans on Contiki's Facebook Page, over 116,000 monthly active users, the creation of over 1,500 virtual buses, and more than 10 million online impressions generated through Facebook shares, Likes, tweets, and coverage from blogs and travel sites.

An increase of 25 percent in total online brand mentions was recorded during the campaign as well as a 24 percent lift in positive brand sentiment. Millions more offline impressions were generated through word-of-mouth, Contiki rep promotions on college campuses, and radio advertising. Contiki also benefited from thousands of potential new customers who arrived through email sign-ups and leads for potential tour bookings.

How A Retailer Ran A Facebook Competition And Hit 3 Million Views Plus $35m In Gift Registry Creation

Ah! And of course, weddings—we cannot forget about weddings. Months, if not years, in the planning, weddings are the perfect event to generate interest and friends' admiration on Facebook.

Home furnishings retailer Crate and Barrel sought to capitalise on its fans' urge to be seen to drive gift registry creation and engage consumers online. For a chance to win a $100,000 dream wedding, Crate and Barrel appealed to newly engaged couples across the U.S. by asking them to create a gift registry with a minimum of $2,000 in products, then submit three images, and answer three questions. Then, a round of public voting and a panel of judges finally picked the grand prize winner and runners-up.

Adhering to Facebook's rule that mandates marketers to host contests on a tab, instead of on their main walls, Crate and Barrel used Strutta's Contest API (Strutta is one of the several companies specialising in running Facebook contests) to validate each couple's gift registry for entry, manage and moderate all content, and provide a link to the couple's gift registry on its entry page.

The contest was promoted across many channels—on Crate and Barrel's websites through press releases and online advertising, through direct e-mail and blogger outreach, as well as in-store displays. Individual stories generated from the contest also gained coverage in local papers, media, and blogs across the country.

The result of such an extremely broad exposure? Three million page views over a year with 500,000 votes each year, 16,000 couples' stories, and $35 million in gift registry sales over two campaigns. Ah! And one very happy couple!

How A Swedish Website Hit 31,000 Fans With Funny Classified Ads

Blocket.se is the largest online website for classified ads in Sweden. With around 4.5 million unique visitors per week, 70 percent of Swedes have bought or sold something on Blocket. Since the website is all about buying and selling, there aren't many opportunities for the company to interact with its users. That's where Facebook comes in.

Blocket decided to run a contest on Facebook with the double goal to increase overall brand awareness and its number of fans. The campaign concept still has Swedes talking about it today: Funny classified ads.

For Blocket, SkandNet designed and developed a contest app and called it "The funniest classified ad on Blocket." The competition ran for seventeen days and had people submitting images of funny classified ads they had noticed on the site. Then Blocket's jury chose twenty finalists while Facebook's users voted for their favourites.

Then it was full on promotion—online banners on Blocket.se, Marketplace Ads on Facebook, blog mentions, newspapers, radio... even the largest Swedish newspaper, *Aftonbladet*, ran the promotion on its website, Aaftonbladet.se, as one of the top news stories.

But what happened next was incredible:

- Over 31,000 new fans in only eighteen days

- Over 34,000 people installed the app

- Over 1,000 daily Likes and comments during the campaign's peak

The story behind the winning classified ad was funny to say the least—a poor old Volvo had been driven into a ditch and the seller wanted the buyer to retrieve it.

Hey! It's worth a try!

Getting 216 Leads For A Professional Services Company Through A Facebook Competition

Last year at E-Web, we ran an online marketing competition using Facebook. We offered a grand prize of over $56,000 worth of online marketing services and training. It was a huge success. For $1,854 spent on advertising, we got over 3 million impressions, 4,009 clicks, and 216 entries. So it was $8.58 per entry. We're a services business, so to get 216 entries at $8.58 a lead is phenomenal.

Here's the landing page we used; feel free to model it for your competitions.

Here's the most successful Facebook ad we ran:

Headline: WIN with E-Web Marketing!

Body: Winning business will receive over 50K of online marketing! Comp ends soon

Five More YouTube Competitions That Went Viral

A sense of humour can go a long way for your business.

Acknowledging that its old jingle needed some revisiting, property and casualty insurance carrier Safe Auto created its YouTube channel, "Legal For Less," and in January 2013, Safe Auto held an open casting call to find the stars of its next ad campaign—a person or a group. Each contestant was to recreate, reinterpret, or reinvent the old Safe Auto Jingle. The winner, selected by the YouTube audience, was to receive $5,000 and would get to appear in a Safe Auto commercial.

The contest generated millions of online votes and helped Safe Auto with web traffic and publicity. Each time a new spot was produced, Safe Auto got the footage from the production house and posted the content on YouTube simultaneously for when each commercial hit the rotation on TV. Placing the proper keywords on each video, promoting the spots on the homepage of its website, and showing off the content to its social media following enabled Safe Auto to get a lot of views, especially for an auto insurance company, in a relatively short timespan.

The winning video, which was turned into a professionally produced commercial, is one of the more popular spots on Safe Auto's YouTube channel in terms of views.

The company also posted articles about its Do The Jingle contestants on its blog throughout the contest's duration. The backstory brought by each musician was great and provided Safe Auto with wonderful content to work on. In its offices, Safe Auto had its most recent commercial playing on a large TV for visitors to see.

Hundreds of musicians entered this contest for multiple reasons, ranging from the money to the exposure. Not everyone could get the first prize, which landed in the hands of Ayanna Lewis with 300,000 votes, but many contestants received a lot of attention from local media.

There's a link to the winning jingle in the free book resources page (http://www.feedastarvingcrowd.com/resources).

The Best Job In The World?

While Tourism Australia's "Best Job in the World" video contest sounded like a joke, it wasn't. The right video and the right personality landed 2012 winner Ben Southall and six other mates a $100,000 a year job in the Great Barrier Reef in 2013.

Ben and his friends' initial application involved a thirty-second video and a test of their ability to generate buzz. The shortlisted few headed to Australia for a one-week test that included reviewing Perth's best restaurants, attending VIP parties and festivals in Sydney, and feeding the kangaroos on Kangaroo Island.

Still sounds like a joke? I know, right?

Nearly 200 competitors hailed from all over the world, but the chief funster job went to American Andrew Smith, who was charged with the "dull" task of instigating fun all over New South Wales, essentially to be a professional partier for six months and then write reviews and tweet about that fun.

But the real winner of this exercise was Australian tourism and the Australian economy. STA Travel reported travel bookings from the U.S. doubled during the contest from what they were a year earlier, while bookings from Germany jumped 42 percent, and bookings from the UK increased 17 percent.

Intel was also pretty generous with the winning prize for its "A Momentary Lapse" competition, a five-month series of photo and video contests held on YouTube to coincide with the launch of its new category of products, the Ultrabook™ inspired by Intel, to fill the gap between lightweight laptops and tablets. With a very tempting $50,000 prize, users were encouraged to create and upload examples of their own slow-motion videos and time lapse photographs and post their entries on the brand's channel MyIntelEdge.

To get their audiences inspired, Intel launched a how-to video with director and photographer Vincent Laforet. The four-minute video was also directly used as a TrueView in-stream ad.

Intel also engaged YouTube content creators who already had a strong following, including Alex Goot, Tyler Ward, and Devin Graham, who has over 800,000 subscribers and 150 million video views. Graham was commissioned to direct a truly inspirational slow-motion video on wingsuit racing for A Momentary Lapse, which was then used as a TrueView ad on YouTube.

The campaign received double the number of expected video submissions—the highest conversion rate from ad to response that the Intel marketing team had ever seen. So given the success, the team extended the YouTube campaign for eight additional weeks. An internal study also saw a brand lift as a result of the campaign.

Clearly, a passionate audience of YouTubers is waiting for a brand to play a bold marketing move, not unlike the one played by Ford in 2009: One hundred cars with petrol and insurance were to be given away to 100 lucky drivers who were to report on their experiences on different social media platforms.

This six-month social media experiment, called "The Ford Fiesta Movement," started with a simple video contest on YouTube and generated a huge amount of buzz. The rules were simple: Upload a video explaining what you would do with a new Ford Fiesta if you were one of the winners.

In just six months, participants posted 11,000 Fiesta-related YouTube videos, and the company tracked more than five million mentions of "Ford Fiesta" or the "Fiesta Movement" across social networking platforms. Without a single dollar spent on traditional advertising, Fiesta experienced:

- a 38 percent boost in awareness of Ford Fiesta among the Gen Y demographic

- 4.8 million views of YouTube videos

- 660,000 views of Flickr photos

- 3.4 million Twitter impressions of the Fiesta Movement

Ford may be a huge brand with the resources to offer huge prizes, but small businesses can host more modest but still successful contests. It just takes the right strategy.

Vlogging Success: How A Shoe Retailer Used Social Tools To Triple Its Sales

Every so often, there's a business that comes on the scene that blows the competition out of the water. It usually has something to do with its innovative marketing tactics that provide a "va-va-voom" foundation. It's this notion that establishes perception and reputation and gets consumers excited and wanting to share and rave to their families and friends. It's kind of like the school ground mentality where the "cool" kids are vying for the leader crown to rule the roost.

Take Shoes of Prey for example. The Australian shoe retailer is so much more than an online store. Its website provides a design interface for customers to create their own pairs of shoes. And the retailer now has its own popup store in David Jones' flagship stores. Its focus lies in providing an experience to customers that'll they'll want to tell their friends about. Stilettos and sparkles aside, Shoes of Prey really pushes the boundaries when it comes to taking risks. Some work, some don't, but the company always learns from the lessons.

For the cofounders of the company, husband and wife duo Michael and Jodie Fox and business partner Mike Knapp, social marketing lies at the business' core. In the short time since its inception, Shoes of Prey has developed some impressive numbers to boast about. There are 190,000 trillion possible amalgamations of shoe designs and women have spent over 60 million minutes designing millions of shoes, Jodie Fox tells us.

But where does all of this hype come from? Is there money and bribery involved?

Enter social media. The brand's Facebook page has a healthy 135,000 following, while its Twitter channel lays claim to 7,400+ followers, and the Instagram platform enjoys a 6,600-strong community base. Facebook drives 4 percent of the brand's traffic and 8 percent of its sales, according to Fox. Shoes of Prey has been able to grow its business into a global spectacle, largely due to the social aspect that has projected the brand onto the world stage. According to Fox, 30 to 40 percent of sales are in Australia. The rest are overseas with about 30 percent from the U.S. and about 20-30 percent from Europe.

Shoes of Prey played with video content long before most other local retailers got on the bandwagon.

In 2010, Shoes of Prey ran a successful YouTube campaign with sixteen-year-old vlogger, Blair Fowler, also known to her followers as "juicystar07." This vlogging sensation was asked to sample a pair of custom-made shoes and review them on her video blog. She also propelled a brand competition to design a pair of shoes through her social channels. What followed was a marketing success story. Blair referred 200,000 visits to the website when it went live, as well as 93,000 competition entries. The video has since had over 750,000 views and more than 95,000 comments. The video was the fifth most viewed on YouTube worldwide during its first week and the most commented on video worldwide for one day.

The link to the video is in the free book resources section (http://www.feedastarvingcrowd.com/resources).

Unfortunately, conversions, which are the vital ingredient for a retail company, weren't so impressive in the first instance. Juicystar07's audience is primarily girls, ages thirteen to seventeen. Their passion lies in shoe design and fashion, but Shoes of Prey presented above its audience's budget capabilities. But the fact that Blair's following can generate a tripling of website visitors in only a couple of days shows the power of new media like YouTube.

Blair was, of course, paid a sum for the original review. Shoes of Prey would not detail what this figure was, but it did state that Blair reviewed the shoes first before agreeing to take payment and create the video, which is housed on her YouTube channel. Shoes of Prey then worked closely with Blair and her agency to implement a competition that would suit her audience and provide ROI for the retailer. Blair promoted the competition to her community, and then she chose the winner.

But Shoes of Prey didn't stop there. The retailer got its marketing hat on and looked at how it could convert these social sharing commodities into actual customers. Here's what it did:

- Recognised the young female demographic was using Facebook and Twitter to converse about the brand. Then it made changes to the website to make it easier for users to share the shoe designs through social networks with obvious social icons displayed prominently on the product pages.

- Conducted Twitter search analysis to discover every conversation about the brand. Then it joined these conversations, engaging with the people personally to garner further feedback and information.

The main aim was to reach the older friends and family members of the women who were generating the original conversations since these women form the brand's target market. Shoes of Prey then shared what it had learnt with a sequence of blog posts about the video competition. The goal was to have the business press pick up the story. It used Twitter to spread the word about the blog post, and the traction that followed was phenomenal. Nearly 100 people retweeted the story with close to 3,000 people viewing the blog post. The story was picked up by leading media outlets including *The Courier Mail*, *The Wall Street Journal* Blog, Business Insider, and a video interview for Sky Business News, as well as international media in China, Sweden, and Germany.

To this day, Shoes of Prey continues to experience good results online, and the retailer's daily sales are now consistently three times higher than they were in the weeks leading up to the video launch. That's a 300 percent uplift in sales. Pretty impressive numbers. These results are not entirely due to the video, though. A lot has to do with a new website redesign and continual updates, but much of the increase is a flow-on effect from the power of online media.

Action Exercise: Choose one campaign case study that feels right for your business and model its success! Run a competition and watch the entries fly in.

9

PLAYING MIND GAMES WITH VIDEO SALES LETTERS

"Agora Publishing has chosen the butt ugly video over the butt ugly sales letter. It's made them a few hundred million dollars."
— **Harlan Kilsetin, copywriter**

Let me start with a brutally biased reference to the best show in TV history: *LOST.*

Fans will remember the moment when a character by the name of Karl, a young man interested in reformed evildoer Ben Linus' daughter, gets locked up in Room 23—that bare space used by the Dharma Initiative to cause amnesia in hostiles by showing them a never-ending flow of fast transitioning images accompanied by disturbingly loud drum-and-bass music....

Well, that's exactly how I felt after watching Jon Benson's Videos: Hypnotised—my will mysteriously held captive by superior forces.

Video Sales Letters (VSLs) have been proven time and again to be one of the highest converting ways of making sales online. Using Jon Benson's video sales letter strategies has generated his clients over $1 billion in sales. (So it's worth reading this chapter.)

A video sales letter turns your traditional long copy sales letter into a video format. In its simplest form, an "ugly duckling" VSL is simply PowerPoint slides, with a white background and black text, with a voiceover reading the text. With a bit more sophistication, there are also "whiteboard videos," "animated videos," and "doodle videos."

Many would call it ugly marketing.

However, let's remind ourselves that ugly does not necessarily mean ineffective. John Benson's VSLs, developed after many years of trying very hard to become an Internet fitness mogul, might be as ugly as they are blunt, but they are methodically crafted to get you to press the "Buy now" button. And many people do.

What's really remarkable here is that if you go to sites that help infopreneurs market their products to niche audiences and advertisers like Clickbank or Commission Junction, a large majority of the top performers among those sites use video sales letters to engage their prospects.

Why? What sort of power do VSLs have that we have all become so hypnotised?

What really matters is the rapport you create through carefully chosen words and the effect these words have on readers and their actions—the emotions you trigger by telling a visual story.

Videos are proven to convert higher, to double or triple conversion rates, if not more. Why? Let's look at the compounding psychological tactics behind VSLs that made me, in the first place, keen to find out more:

Compulsion To Read On

Watching a video takes a lot less effort than reading a letter or a website. Videos also engage more senses than texts do so people will read every single word in VSLs rather than skimming through the content in your site because in a way, their senses give them no choice. The lack of visual clutter plus (in Jon's words) "ninja psychological sales copy," compels them to read along with the narrator, just like they read along when Mum and Dad read them a bedtime story during their childhood. Unlike ordinary sales pages where only a small percentage of the copy is read—mostly the heading and the price paid—VSLs use various modalities to maximise viewer attention through an almost hypnotic effect of fast-moving slides that compel audiences to engage fully in the text before them.

Modality Marketing

VSLs cleverly play with both sensory (sound, sight, touch…) and learning modalities (avoid, enjoy, and how-to), using them as powerful subconscious controllers. But because everyone has different modalities, different ways to perceive the world, marketers need to cover all bases and deliver as many strong sensory and learning modalities as possible in order to build rapport with most customers. For instance, you can't merely rely on listening modalities like:

When you hear the amazing benefits of…

Or

Listen to customers' rave reviews

because you are alienating customers who prefer other modality types like feel, think, see, or even taste! Take this for an example:

"You know, I used to feel as if I had to think about every word of my sales copy until I listened to…."

Here, you've used various sensory modalities—knowing, feeling, thinking, and listening—reflecting the vocabulary customers utilise to make sense of their everyday world, to perceive the environment around them. In doing so, you have successfully established a connection with them; you've built that emotional rapport that is crucial for them to trust you.

Meet The Reluctant Hero

Below, I've shared some examples of copy used in VSLs I've watched recently. All of them use the very same formula to establish rapport with the prospect—the reluctant hero formula: "Hey, look at me; I'm not that different from you; I was no one at one point—in debt, close to bankruptcy, ashamed, confused…." And they go on telling a dramatic visual story that feeds from everyone's love for tragedy. But it gets worse. The modest hero hits rock bottom. But then, that one magic day. Things start to change.

And we, the listener/reader, we know that this journey is somewhat cheesy and definitely formulaic, and yet, we are glued. Reluctant heroes are people magnets. People want to know their stories and want to believe that one day, that formula will apply to them too. Here are examples of how they grab our attention:

> Hi, my name is Mike and I'm not one of those flashy gurus who appear at the big events. I'm a guy like you who was struggling for years to make my own products sell well. And after seven years of misery, I am happy to admit that I found out how to do it!

> Or

> Before we get started, I just want you to know that I am not a world-class copywriter. I pretty much stink at traditional sales letters. But, I have found a very effective formula for creating highly-converting video sales letters. So that means that you can do this too. There are no superhuman abilities required here. You simply follow the formula I'm about to teach you and get results that are USUALLY reserved for highly-paid copywriters.

Jon Benson was the first person ever to create a VSL. After generating over $1 billion in sales for his clients, he now sells a VSL generator that automatically creates a VSL for you based on your product. (I've got a link for his site and some examples of his work in the free book resources section: http://www.feedastarvingcrowd.com/resources). Here's his story:

> I never wanted to be a copywriter; I wanted to be a musician, but I started online and in the fitness industry about ten years ago, and it was then that some things transpired. I'm a kid from Brooklyn, New York, my father having worked a manual job all his life. I owe my work ethic to my father, but I had no advantages when I started my online business. I have degrees in philosophy and music and zero Internet skills except for those I picked up in my failed online venture when I was thirty. Not only that, I was an obese man with heart disease. I didn't know what I wanted to be until I was forty years old. I struggled first with copywriting like most business owners do. Then one day, everything changed for me. I was doing YouTube videos to promote my own products, and I would be lucky to get ten sales from a video that took hours or days to prepare.
>
> It was a Saturday night and I had to do yet another YouTube video; my favourite game was playing. I was reading a book about psychology that dealt with how we best absorb information. One study said that we pay more attention and remain engaged longer when reading and listening at the same time. That was it. That led me to create a billion dollar marketing vehicle while watching my team, sitting in my boxer shorts. That day I decided to put big black words in a white background on a PowerPoint presentation and highlighted specific words that needed to be trigger words—words that drive action, promote curiosity, increase engagement. Then I put that five-minute video on YouTube and emailed it to my list promoting my underwhelming business.

That video converted just under 1 percent and that means for every 100 people that hit my site, about seven people bought it, and then, that was considered to be good!

I had to look at my stats twice and then decided to make the entire video longer, eighteen minutes, and I split-tested it against my text-based sales page. Conversions went up to 6.1 percent, a 600 percent increase in conversions.

That ugly VSL outsold my classy video by 600 percent. In nine months, I became the largest selling digital marketer online.

You can use formulas in many different ways throughout your VSL, not just in your introduction or to build up your persona. For instance, Jon recommends always to keep to this flow of events:

Step 1: Initial Snap Suggestion That Hooks Your Prospects' Attention

When potential customers start watching your VSL, they are generally immersed in different states of mind, from frustration to anticipation. You need to interrupt this pattern, to neutralise their thoughts and get their full attention.

Jon says that getting people's full attention is the most important part of the VSL because people are coming from different traffic sources and they are very easily distracted. If you don't grab their attention in the first few slides, there's a huge chance they will bounce off your site and you've lost them forever.

The best testing results will come from playing with the first ten slides.

The Truth About Abs is one of the most successful fitness products on the market today. Mike Geary, the product creator, consistently sells over $1 million per month in product sales—just by using a Video Sales Letter—and he only has one product, which sells for $47!

Of course, I've analysed this video in detail, and I have some great insights for you below.

In the truthaboutabs VSL (www.truthaboutabs.com), the first slide is a massive pattern interrupt—if you're a woman who wants a flat stomach (I'm pretty sure that applies to a large percentage of the population!)—there's a big chance you'll keep reading. Also because the text is handwritten and untidy, and there is a hand-drawn image of the woman on the right, it's so "unpolished" that you can't help but wonder what's coming up next!

Step 2: Creating Rapport, A Vital Connection

As we have seen, most authors will establish a connection by making prospects identify with them through the tragic stories of their lives; others might tell them why they are qualified to provide the information they are about to get.... Remember, we buy from people we relate to.

Another example is in the truthaboutabs VSL. Here's where you show that you're actually not that different from the reader:

Hi, I'm Jon. I'm not a naturally lean guy; in fact, I was down-right obese for many, many years. And when I found out that it wasn't my fault, well that was one of the best days of my life. I'm going to tell you my story because it's probably very similar to your own. It doesn't matter if you're a guy or a gal; anyone who struggles with their weight and their waistline will relate to this story.

Step 3: The Big Problem

As a marketer, the next thing you need to do is show that the problem the viewer faces is actually bigger than he or she thinks. The bigger the problem, the more likely the viewer is to buy. In my corporate career, I was always taught to "build the pain." Actually, I distinctly remember being shown a see-saw, with pain on one side and buyer resistance on the other. The stronger the pain, the lower the buyer resistance!

The big question is obviously: "How do you build this pain?"

Here's an example in the truthaboutabs VSL:

> If you're anything like me, you've probably been beating your head against the wall for years, maybe even decades, all because you do not have that flat, firm stomach you long for. I remember the first time that I saw abs on someone. I was in the seventh grade. We were in the locker room after football practice. Now I knew my friend Joey had "that" body. You know, the one that girls loved and that guys wanted to have, but I never knew he had "that"—great abs. I mean a firm, super tight midsection that just made me want to go home and do a thousand sit-ups and guess what I did. I was really sore the next day, so sore I couldn't even practice.

Here's another example of Jon amping up the pain in the truthaboutabs:

> Sure, Joey had great genetics; no one else in the locker room had those abs that's for sure, but come on, I was lying to myself. Now I'm an honest guy, so admitting this was very, very difficult, and the fact that I was lying to myself didn't hit me all

of a sudden. After all, I had tried dieting; I'd done sit-ups and crunches for years. The only thing I managed to do was pull my back muscles and trim my waistline by about an inch, maybe two at the most, but not an ab muscle in sight. My clothes were always uncomfortable on me, and I never wanted to take my shirt off at the beach or at the pool. In essence, I was like a prisoner in my own body.

My mind wanted something that at least I believed my body could never give me. Maybe this sounds like someone you know; maybe it sounds just like you.

Step 4: The Bigger Solution

The next step is to show the solution because if you build up a problem without a solution, the viewer will not believe there is a solution available.

If you train your abs directly too much you're just going to build the muscles underneath your layer of fat. Now that's great if you want a bigger stomach and that's not what most of us want. Not only that, but direct ab exercises can cause your body to go into a state of what we call, "over training." This wears you out and makes you not want to go to the gym, not want to work out. It can even ruin your enthusiasm for dieting.

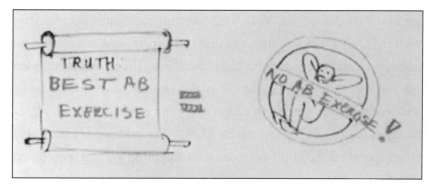

Step 5: The Grand Offer

Now it's time to introduce the offer:

> Well, I want to introduce you to a friend of mine, a professional ab expert, Mike Geary. He's a world-renowned professional trainer; he's also a certified nutrition specialist. His principles are tried, tested, and proven, not by dozens but by hundreds and thousands of people, just like you and me. Mike's best-selling program, "The Truth about Six Pack Abs" is exactly that—the truth about getting six pack abs. In fact, to date, over 263,000 people in 154 countries have used the Truth about Abs program already.

Each of these steps has a lot more copy in it; I've just given you the introductory copy for each of the sections. To get a more detailed outline, I'd recommend you look further into Jon's 3xVSL formula, and his 3xVSL generator, which actually generates these video sales letters for you! Check the free book resources page (http://www. feedastarvingcrowd.com/resources) for the most recent link to these products.

More VSL Tips And Tricks

A common question to ask is whether it's best to use an Ugly Duckling text only VSL or go all the way and use a whiteboard video, like you see in the truthaboutabs VSL. Jon's recommendation is simple. Start with the Ugly Duckling first, get that converting, and then test out a whiteboard video against the Ugly Duckling. The whiteboard video can improve conversions, and it can also reduce conversions. It's not a silver bullet. You need to test it for your market. Also, a whiteboard video can cost as much as $1,000 per minute to create. No point spending $20,000 or more on something you haven't tested yet. That's crazy.

How about voiceovers? Do you read it yourself or get a professional? Jon's recommendation is to read it yourself, although professional voiceovers can also get good results.

When you are sending traffic to the video, use "free presentation" instead of "free video." Free presentation means the video is loaded with valuable, stand-alone content.

On the VSL video player, you want to have no player controls. No rewinding or fast forwarding. They've gotta watch the video the whole way through to see everything. I know this sounds annoying, but this has been tested comprehensively. When you put player controls on, conversion drops dramatically.

Auto-play converts higher than "click to play." Again, I know this is annoying from a user experience perspective, but you gotta do what converts better!

Only show the "Magic buy button" when the sales pitch starts. Before that, you want to give the impression that this is simply a free presentation to watch. If you show the offer from the start, people will click-through to see the price and not watch the presentation.

Here is an example of the industry standard, best-practice layout of a VSL page.

Action Exercise: It's time to produce your first VSL! Go through the steps that Jon has formulated and give it a crack.

10

CROWD FUNDING, OR HOW DESPERATELY TO SHOW THEM YOU ARE UNIQUE

"The poor man who enters into a partnership with one who is rich makes a risky venture."

— Plautus

I don't drink coffee liqueur. In fact, I don't even like coffee liqueur, and yet only yesterday, I was tempted to invest $50 on the best cold drip coffee liqueur in the world.

Why was I about to part with $50?

Because Mr. Black's makers, a new business venture hoping to crowd fund $10,000 to produce its first batch of this "deliciously black liquid," told a story I felt I had to reward, a story of hard work and perseverance, a well told story. Today, I received an email from Mr. Black saying that it had reached the pledged amount at the Australian crowd funding site Pozible in only thirteen days. And interest in Mr. Black keeps on growing.

Good for Mr. Black.

Three Examples Of Companies Using Crowd Funding To Raise $1 Million In 24 Hours

But let's think bigger numbers. Here are a couple of success stories:

9 February, 2012—Portland's Casey Hopkins breaks the million dollar barrier in crowd funding platform Kickstarter with an elevated iPhone dock. Only a few hours later, computer game developers Double Fine Productions hoping to collect $400,000 for a new 2D adventure, reached their funding goal in less than nine hours of their month-long drive. Within 24 hours, Double Fine Adventure had raised more than a million dollars, becoming the most funded and most backed project ever on Kickstarter. They finished up with over $3 million.

6 March, 2013—inXile Entertainment's game *Torment: Tides of Numenera* was successfully crowd funded through Kickstarter in the first six hours of the 30 day project's launch, surpassing Obsidian Entertainment's Project Eternity as the most funded video game in this site with a total of $4,188,927 pledged by 74,405 backers.

Not all crowd funding success stories are about fun and games. Inma Zamora explains that Arcanum Project managed to gather more than the amount pledged thirty days before the deadline at Spanish site Lanzanos for its "biological computer." The money has been invested in purchasing the equipment needed to modify bacteria genetically, have the information processed, and return a result, as your computer would. Not my cup of tea, but hey, the guy raised 130,000 Euros in twenty days!

Come On; Is It Really All That Simple?

Is it just a matter of presenting a fairly well-developed concept, wrapping it up in eye-catching packaging, and waiting for interested investors to respond to your pledge?

Not so lucky. It isn't merely about posting a half-thought-out idea on some online platform, walking away, and coming back a month later to find $10,000 magically waiting in your bank account. "Forty-four percent of the campaigns launched on Pozible fail," explains crowd funding connoisseur James Lees, "because people don't run their campaigns properly, they don't pitch their campaigns properly, and they're not capturing the goodwill of their potential supporters."

So, how do you entice a "starving crowd" of like-minded individuals to invest directly in your start-up in exchange for equity in your new big idea? How do you, in this seemingly endless wave of recession, entice cash-rich donors to give you, and only you, a chance at success?

Let's find the common denominators in the success.

What Makes A Crowd-Funding Campaign Successful?

In an interview with Kickstarter, Brian Fargo—video game designer, producer, and founder of developers Interplay Entertainment and InXile Entertainment—explains he had been dreaming about making a sequel to his popular 1983 game *Wasteland* for over twenty years. In that period, he invested a great deal of time and effort trying to find backers through the usual financing means, but he got nowhere. Brian knew exactly how much support he needed, how he'd use the funds raised, how long it would take him to complete the project, and what the cost of marketing would be. He knew his project like the back of his hand, and he was frustrated about not being able to get the support he deserved.

But his fans were relentless. They wanted a new game from Brian. They wanted a sequel to *Wasteland* one way or another. So Brian turned to crowd funding, or in his case, fan funding. On the 6th of March 2013, Brian was very nervous. Nothing else had worked and there really were no guarantees this would work either, but he was hoping to make $900,000.

Why $900,000, you might ask? How did Brian know what was the magic figure that would set him and his team off? Brian put it very simply to the guys at PCgamesN: "We knew what kind of experience we wanted to deliver and we just had to do it for the minimum amount of money." It was partly psychological too, a statement from Brian telling fans, "You guys put up nine hundred thousand, I'll put up the other hundred, I'm in this too."

That day there was a lot at stake.

Brian was up at 5:30, he recounts. Fans were asking him on Twitter when he was going to go live. He knew there was some anticipation. His pre-campaign launch video updates talking about the process, the concept, and the team had certainly helped.

An earlier milestone in February also boosted Brian's chances. The Torment team took a snapshot of itself playing the actual game. The team waited until the game was organically ready and correct and then captured about fifteen minutes of gameplay. This preview gave backers a little taste of things to come—the interface, the style, the graphics, the combat systems, the nuances, the use of skills, and so on. People loved it. Brian tells us at PCgamesN that people absolutely loved it. In fact, he adds, "I wouldn't have launched the Torment Kickstarter if they didn't love that, but they did."

He also produced a strong video for Kickstarter with two significant components—a human narrative depicting the great people on his team, their aspirations, dreams, and above all, their devotion to the game industry. On the other hand, superior concept art with a lot of detail gave fans a really good idea of what they were getting. The video was almost seven minutes long and most people later told Brian they "didn't even watch the whole video. [They] donated right away. They were stopping in the middle."

In forty-three hours, Brian reached his goal. His final pledge exceeded $4 million.

Brian's decade-long experience in the field made him an almost instant winner—he knew the state of the industry, he knew there was a gap that the fans wanted filled, and he knew he had the credibility to fill it.

Five Key Elements To Get Investors To Pull Out Their Wallets And Fund Your Campaign

1. Write a memorable headline

Something striking like "Throw trucks with your mind" will work, although a less fictional title with an interesting hook will also do the trick.

2. Tell an engaging story

It's everybody's ocean is the story of the residents of the tiny island of Ikema, Japan, a popular destination for tourists, which is now facing the threat of large amounts of marine debris from all over Asia. This is a good story because it not only raises awareness of Ikema's struggles, but it also casts a light on the wider issue of marine waste, an issue that affects us all. Give your audience something that binds it to your narrative. Tell a transparent story that tells people who you are, why you started this project, what your goals are, and how you plan to succeed.

The honesty I felt in Mr. Black's video is what made me want to part with my $50.

3. Produce an unforgettable video

Remember, your video is the focal point of your campaign. The video's purpose is to show—not just tell, show—people what you plan to do, the value-added of the product and the team's passion. Give them product demos, interviews, infographics, slideshows, and any visuals that are compelling and help tell your story.

The video is your only chance to connect face-to-face with your supporters so remain true to yourself and try to sum up your message in a clear, concise, and personal way. And do it fast (the Suitcase Entrepreneur, www.SuitcaseEntrepreneur. com, has shown that people know whether they are going to support the project in the first minute of the video).

4. Give your backers rewards that are truly worth their while

How about your backer's face on a bus travelling with the band Foster the People around the USA to support local non-profits? Yes, why not. It would be very much like what the Do Good Bus does. The bus takes a load of people, goes out to areas in need, and the whole bus helps out with the good cause. The Do Good Bus offered you the chance to "get your face on the bus" if you backed them on the crowdfunding site Start Some Good (startsomegood.com). It was a very successful campaign, raising $100,000 with contributions from 680 backers ranging from $1 to over $10,000.

5. Find the social media platform that best suits your purpose

Facebook is great, but it's not your only ally. Rebecca Pontius, who led the initial effort at the Do Good Bus, says, "it took consistent monitoring, posts on Twitter and Facebook, personal begging emails to friends and support from the band to raise the money in time." The Do Good Bus played the Twitter card fairly strongly by partnering with Start Some Good for its #StartingGood Twitter conversation about crowd funding and starting social good.

An Unusual Startup Campaign That Raised $2.1m In The Blink Of An Eye

An Angelist startup campaign that caught my eye was Shyp, a shipping business that picks up parcels from homes and businesses and places them with the cheapest shipping option available. Neat! I imagine the founders had a significant number of logistical hurdles to overcome, but I've had some chats with the founders and they are very intelligent guys. I have no doubt that they will be successful.

Side note, I love Shyp's web design. If you ever want to get a great example of user experience design that is clean and gets to the point, check out www.shyp.com. I was so excited when I first saw it, and I grabbed my colleagues Adrian and Dino and said "LOOK AT THIS! LOOK HOW GOOD THIS IS!" If Mike (Shyp co-founder) had a twin brother who lived in Australia, I would have hired him yesterday.

Okay, let's get back to raising money.

What makes Shyp any different or better than other startups?

The investors they've got on board:

- Tim Ferriss (NYT best-selling author)

- David Marcus (President of PayPal)

- Brian McClendon (Founder of Google Earth)

- Daymond John (Founder of FUBU, Shark on ABC's *Shark Tank*)

- Joshua Schachter (Founder of Delicious, Tasty Labs)

- Aaron Batalion (Cofounder of LivingSocial)

- Homebrew (Hunter Walk and Satya Patel)

- Naval Ravikant (CEO/cofounder of AngelList)

- Scott Belsky (Founder and CEO of Behance)

- Sherpa Ventures (Scott Stanford and Shervin Pishevar)

- Antonio J. Gracias (Board Member at Tesla and SolarCity)

- XG Ventures (Andrea Zurek and Pietro Dova)

- Osama Bedier (Former head of Google Wallet)

How did they get these investors onboard? I have never seen investors of this calibre all get onboard at the same time. I'll answer that, but first, let me explain how I found out about these guys.

Easy. I got an email from Tim Ferriss encouraging me to be an investor. Tim Ferriss and I have a special relationship. He emails me once a week or so and lets me know what he's up to. (He also emails 1.4m other people the same message.)

What is most interesting is that Tim blasted his whole list about this investment opportunity. As long as someone is an "accredited investor" (read: earning over $200k/year and meeting some other criteria), they can now be email blasted about upcoming deals. Previously you needed to be "in the know" to hear about these deals. Not anymore.

I was actually quite keen to invest with these guys; however, I was too slow. I received the email from Tim at 2 a.m. on Wednesday morning. At 7 a.m. I checked my email and clicked on the link and found that the funding was closed off because Shyp had met its funding target.

What? I hit "refresh" in my browser to double-check that it wasn't an error.

Nope, no error.

So, Tim Ferriss sold out $250,000 of investor funding in less than five hours. Actually, reading some press coverage after the fact, I learned it was actually fifty-three minutes.

Greg Kumparak from TechCrunch proposes that this is how Shyp raised $2.1 million in funding:

- $1.35m of it came from more traditional fundraising sources (led by Hunter Walk's Homebrew and Sherpa Ventures, backed by a bevy of Angels)

- Tim Ferriss privately raised $500,000 of it from his own contacts. Some of the investors in that chunk include Antonio J. Gracias (Board of Directors on both SpaceX/Tesla) and Daymond John (FUBU founder, and one of the *Shark Tank* sharks)

- That leaves $250,000, which is what they set aside to raise through general solicitation on AngelList by way of a Tim Ferriss blog post.

Wow.

Being a naturally curious person, I got in touch with Shyp's founders and asked, "How did you do this?" They replied, "Oh we got a few investors on board and we're really happy with them."

Understatement of the century, right?

Me, being the prying investigative author, of course, dug deeper.

Me: Can you tell me exactly how you got those investors onboard?

Shyp: We found AngelList to be a great platform by which to get our first investors onboard. Then we also got intros to investors from people we knew whom they'd previously funded. Finally, once we had initial investors on board, we asked them for referrals to other investors that we wanted. We didn't know any of these guys prior to getting funded by them.

They didn't know any of these guys prior to getting funding? What were their tips and tricks?

Shyp: With AngelList it's important to build a solid profile across all the areas, fill it out fully. Then time the timing of when you push it live carefully. You want to get traction in a short amount of time, not spread out. So maybe list on AngelList after you already get one investor committed. Then ask all your friends to follow it, so you get incremental traction, etc.

So let's look at their AngelList page, where all the magic happened. It's followed best practice in filling out its investment profile page:

1. Informative two-minute video trailer with high production value

2. Traction and social proof—It's already shipped 250 packages and has customer testimonials on the site

3. Founders information: Jack Smith was the co-founder of Vungle, a mobile ad platform, and that has enjoyed $8.5 million of investor funding

What Are The Common Denominators Of A Successful Crowd-Funding Campaign?

Nearly excessive amounts of passion and creativity, undoubtedly excessive amounts of dedication and perseverance, and a good dash of credibility. All of them backed by an engaging narrative that appeals to potential angels, and add a big chunk of your time.

Fingers crossed!

Action Exercise: It's time for you to have a crack at crowd funding! Think about a product, service, or cause you'd like to promote, build a page, get a video online, and get the word out!

11

GETTING YOUR BOOK ON THE BEST-SELLER LIST

On August 1, 2012, I set myself a goal of being a best-selling author by the end of November 2012. I procrastinated for three weeks; then I thought I should do something about this goal if I'm going to achieve it! I procrastinated for another few weeks and only got serious about putting together the book outline in mid-September. From then, I went into over-drive, and I wrote the book, had it edited, formatted, and published on Amazon in two months. It was called *Email Marketing that Sells: Your guide to building a fired up email list.*

How My First Book Got To The Best-Seller List Without Using Book Tours Or Expensive PR

The main recipes for success were the two weeks of hype and build up before the launch, multiple promotions to our list, the Facebook ads, and the loyal launch team members who promoted the book to their networks. What also worked quite well was a Facebook "offer" that over 150 people claimed, and it went virally into their newsfeeds.

What's The "Book Launch Team"?

One of the key reasons for my success was developing a "book launch" team. I learnt this idea from Michael Hyatt, author of *The Platform*. You ask people if they'd like to read a "pre-launch" copy of your book, in return for writing a review and promoting the book launch to their friends. This was a great idea, although you can't count on every person on your launch team to be as excited about your book as you are. In my case, I had over 100 people who said they wanted to be on my launch team, but only ten people actually ended up contributing. And I don't blame them for not taking action; they've probably got higher priorities than promoting my book, but it was a massive learning for me that you can't take your launch team for granted.

In the free book resources section, I've included the exact emails and campaign sequence I used to help get the book launch team onboard.

What Went Wrong?

At 5 p.m. on Friday (just before launch), I realised we were in the wrong Amazon Kindle categories. Sigh. All of the time and effort we put into choosing the right categories would be wasted if this situation were not fixed. So I quickly had to change the categories and hold my breath while Amazon implemented the changes on its end. To say I was nervous was an understatement, especially when the message said it would take up to twelve hours to update! Thankfully, Amazon updated the changes almost immediately and the launch went off without a hitch. Be careful when you choose your categories because the physical book categories don't match up to the Kindle book categories.

I also felt our launch day execution could have been better coordinated to get more downloads in a shorter period of time. Again, this was a lesson for me and an area where I have continued to improve with each book launch. Getting to best-selling author means you need a twenty-four-hour hard slog of promotion because you want everyone to download the book on the same day. My downloads were spread out relatively evenly over five days. Although I still achieved my goal of getting to best-selling author, I'll certainly be a lot more organised next time, and I'll have closer relationships with my launch team to coordinate promoting to their audiences at the same time.

How To Get Reviews

My team collated a list of the top 500 Amazon reviewers and approached each of them to review my first book about email marketing. There were three who said yes, and only one actually went ahead and did it. It's a hard slog getting reviews from people you don't know.

An easier way is to ask business acquaintances, people you know, journalists, and fellow authors. What works best is the law of reciprocity. You should review another author's book first before asking him or her to review yours.

This is the way I got many of my book reviews. Once the book is live, then you also get reviews from randoms who have bought it as well, which is cool (and scary).

Another #1 Amazon Best-Seller Story

Joseph Assaf uttered his first words in Arabic, undertook his schooling in French, migrated to an English speaking country, married an Italian, and became involved in the business of communicating to a multicultural audience.

In 1967, at the age of twenty-two, without speaking English and having no money or family, Joseph migrated to Australia from Lebanon in someone else's shoes. Upon arrival, he worked in a factory at night and studied during the day.

In 1977, Joseph pioneered multicultural communication.

In 1988, Joseph founded and continues to run the Ethnic Business Awards, which celebrate the diversity and multiculturalism of Australia, through immigrants and their businesses.

Joseph's amazing story is detailed in his wonderful book, *In Someone Else's Shoes*.

Last year, E-Web Marketing approached Joseph to take his book, convert it to Kindle format, and sell it on Amazon.

Being the overachiever that I am, I was determined to make this great book a best-seller.

How? Same process as I used for my book, but this time with a larger launch team and more hands-on management. We had 250 people on the launch team and a dedicated launch team manager who kept in very close contact with the launch team.

We also organised a live event "launch party" where we invited selected key influencers who could spread the message across their large networks. This approach worked very well, and over 130 people actually mailed for us on launch day. Score! (Note to self: Stay very close to the launch team).

With these tactics, E-Web Marketing got Joseph Assaf's *In Someone Else's Shoes* to be the #1 marketing book in the whole of Amazon.com and it stayed #1 in the categories of marketing, global marketing, and international marketing for several days.

How James Altucher Sold Books By The Truckload

You may have heard of James Altucher before. If you haven't, he's the author of the book *Choose Yourself*. He's sold a truckload of books and was kind enough to share a few of the tactics that worked really well for him. Here's what he recommends:

1. He set up a Reddit "Ask me anything" page. It got over a million views and 3,000 comments. When you read this page, it's raw and cuts to the heart of why James wrote the book.

2. His PR company Brasscheck (run by Ryan Holiday) organised sixty podcasts, radio interviews, speaking engagements, and guest posts on popular blogs and websites.

3. Brasscheck also created a SlideShare presentation that got 300,000 views. After creating the SlideShare, James promoted the presentation by Facebook and Twitter to get it to the front page. Once on the front page, the organic views took over.

4 *Choose Yourself* was the first book ever pre-sold on Bitcoin. This was newsworthy and Brasscheck ensured the media knew about it. (I noticed that BusinessInsider was very curious about the bitcoin strategy and gave James a solid interview article—nice!)

5. James offered to pay people back for the price of the book if they didn't enjoy it, a full money back guarantee—even if you bought it from a retailer. This means James would lose money on the transaction because he refunds the full price of the book, where he would only receive a smaller commission from the book seller (e.g. Amazon). Big risk! Here's why he says he did it:

"I also wanted to market an offer in the beginning of the book. My goal was not to necessarily make the most money but to make sure the message reached as many people as possible. So on the very first page, before the editorial information and dedication, there is 'the offer.'

"I offer to pay people back for the book if they could prove to me that they bought it and read it. Then I would pay them back completely for the book (losing money on each transaction because of the cut Amazon takes plus shipping). The idea was I would be happy to give the book for free, but I know people don't value things they get for free. And I also know most people don't read the books they buy. Hence the offer."

Again, this helped with publicity, and I'm sure that the refund rate would be quite low—really, who's bothered to send back a $20 book for a refund? But the extra publicity would be well worth the money he would have to pay back. Brilliant.

6. James used a foreign rights agency to handle all of the book's foreign rights on a commission-only basis. And at the time of writing, James already had made $10,000 USD from foreign rights sales—that's great revenue that he didn't have before!

7. This is probably the best—he teamed up with the financial newsletter guru Porter Stansberry and put together a bundle of the new book, three versions of James' past books, plus a special report. Porter emailed this offer to his list with some of the best copywriting I have ever seen (it's 5,000 words of copy for a $23.95 sale.) And Stansberry threw in a three-month free access to his Radio premium product. Just by emailing this offer to his list, Stansberry sold over 20,000 of these packages. Talk about selling books by the truckload!

The Way One Of The World's Highest Selling Authors Chooses Book Titles…That Guarantees They Are Surefire Winners

It's important to test headlines using PPC ads. James Altucher had ten different potential titles for his book, but after doing some Facebook ads, he found the clear winner was *Choose Yourself*. Tim Ferriss used this same strategy with Google AdWords ads for *The 4-Hour Workweek*.

How A BlogPalooza Helped Sell A Million Books

John Kremer, the author of *1001 Ways to Market Your Book*, was recently inspired by Amanda Hocking to name a certain kind of blog tour a "BlogPalooza." He created the term based on a successful blog tour Hocking, an author of zombie novels, had named a

"Zombiepalooza." Before her Zombiepalooza, Hocking had been selling about 3,000-5,000 copies of Kindle ebooks each month, for a total of about 20,000 books before her October 2010 event. Within two months of the event, she more than doubled her monthly sales to 100,000 copies in December, and in January, she sold 450,000 ebooks.

In February 2011, Hocking made the *USA Today* bestseller list. By March, her book sales totaled over 1 million copies and she sold the rights to four of her books for $2 million to St. Martin's Press. Although some people questioned this decision, Hocking wanted to become a billion-dollar author so she partnered with St. Martin's to get her books into stores like Wal-Mart.

Hocking's strategies to create her Zombiepalooza are what created her success. She invited people to write guest-posts on her website and offer their own books for free. These guest bloggers became her fan club, and they in turn, brought their fan clubs to her website, creating greater exposure for Amanda's books and adding to her readership. Her Zombiepalooza got people interested and led to word-of-mouth ebook sales, making it a tremendous success.

Final Tips For Selling A Truckload Of Books

This is not a chapter about how to write a book. I'm assuming you've already written the book and had it formatted, and want to sell a lot of copies and build up a lot of hype.

One thing though: It's no good building hype if your book isn't up to scratch. I want to share with you a couple of tips about what to put into the book to make it a world-class effort.

1. Patrick Snow, bestselling author of *Creating Your Own Destiny* and *The Affluent Entrepreneur*, taught me this one. Each chapter heading is a lesson you want the reader to learn. Your Table of Contents is your sales page, so focus here on interesting,

catchy headlines. You can look at any of the headlines in this book as examples!

2. Always have calls to action scattered throughout the book, encouraging people to download checklists, tips, templates, and extra content back on your website. You can even offer PDF reports, free videos—whatever it takes to get an opt-in! There's no point selling a million copies of the book if you don't build an email list for the future.

Action Exercise: If writing a book is a passion for you, get started today. Once you've finished writing it, you can use the strategies I've shared in this chapter to sell your books by the truckload!

12

INTERESTING AND UNUSUAL PRODUCT LAUNCHES

"Advertising is a tax for having an unremarkable product."
— **Robert Stephens**

Mindvalley Reveals Its Exact Blueprint For Its Famous $1 Million Launch

Mindvalley is the among the world's best in launching new information products. Founder and CEO Vishen Lakhiani and his team of over 100 people are always on the cutting edge of new launch strategies and tactics. It seems like they are continually ahead of the curve while most other online marketers are running fast just to catch up.

After a month of playing email tag, I finally managed to track down Ewa Wysocka, who is the brains behind Mindvalley's Product Launches. Originally from Poland, Ewa believes coming from a non-Western country has actually been an advantage in selling information products to the West. An advantage because she doesn't make any assumptions about the culture and what the market wants.

Let me explain.

Before Mindvalley agrees to launch a product to market, it goes through a rigorous market analysis. It analyses the keywords using Google's keyword tool to see what the traffic volumes are like. It does a Google search to see how competitive the keyword is for SEO. It looks at who's advertising in the market and how sophisticated their advertising is.

Interestingly, Mindvalley breaks up its product set into "front end" and "back end" products. The front end products are mainstream products that many people are searching for, which makes initial customer acquisition much easier. The "back end" products are the ones that people aren't necessarily searching for, but they would be interested in the products if they were presented to them in the right light.

Another way to think of this scenario is that the front end products are "pull marketing" and the back end products are "push marketing."

The Mindvalley launch of Christie Marie Sheldon's Unlimited Abundance course generated over $1 million. Ewa explained that the launch came in two stages: first it launched to the internal Mindvalley list, and then it went out to affiliates.

The launch followed a three-step content marketing process. However, this wasn't just your regular video launch. Each step was carefully planned to be unique and different.

Video 1 was a paradigm shift. Jon Benson would call this a pattern interrupt. The title of the video was "Are You a Lauren or Diane?"

This video showed the twenty-four mindset blocks that stop people from achieving financial abundance. One of the girls had the blocks, and another girl didn't have the mindset blocks. This is brilliant marketing because most of the target market would identify with the girl who had the limiting belief mindsets. Love it!

Video 2 was a "behind the scenes" live client session. Christie sat down with a client and ran a coaching session. The reason for doing this was to build Christie's credibility with the audience and show that Christie was someone who could deliver results.

Content Piece #3 was delivering results in advance. The way Ewa arranged this was brilliant. Everyone has been banging the "webinar" drum so it reached the point of saturation, especially in the information marketing business. What Ewa organised was an "energy clearing session" called "Unblocking Your Abundance" with Christie. What makes this so brilliant is that the "energy clearing session" was simply a webinar, just renamed to sound more holistic!

And the brilliance showed in the results: 30,000 registered to attend the session and 10,000 showed up. Many of the participants reported really feeling the energy of the session, and Mindvalley quickly sold out the first 200 spots (applying scarcity), released another 200 spots, and sold them out too.

A couple of more interesting facts:

1. Each launch page and piece of content was optimised for Facebook sharing. Ewa found that 30 percent of traffic, sign ups, and sales came from the social media shares.

2. The sales page is literally a work of art. It actually doesn't feel like a sales page. There's an infographic on there, video testimonials, an interactive income calculator, frequently asked questions, and a slider showing all of the course content.

I highly recommend you check it out: http://www.unlimitedabundance.com/products

How A Multi-Million Dollar Sales Training National Tour Sold Out—Without Spending A Cent On Advertising

Kerwin Rae achieved the amazing feat of selling out a national seminar tour without paying for any advertising.

Not that there wasn't plenty of advertising for this event—it was advertised on every major TV station and radio network. It was advertised on taxis, billboards going to and from the airport, and in full-page newspaper ads.

But none of this advertising was paid for with hard cash.

And boy did the advertising work. Kerwin filled 5,500 paid seats across four cities in Australia, more than doubling the sales trainer's previous result.

All right. How did he do this?

Being the curious marketer that I am, I interviewed Kerwin and asked him to break this strategy down into the specific steps he followed. The interview was too long to publish in this book, so I've included it in the free book resources section (http://www.feedastarvingcrowd. com/resources).

Tim Ferriss—Using BitTorrent To Launch A New Book

This is Tim Ferriss' story of achieving the kind of success most of us spend our whole lives dreaming of.

Yes, admittedly Tim has always been one gifted and motivated individual—skilled at wrestling, national champion in Chinese kickboxing, adventurer, and unconventional thinker. His abilities and qualities finally landed him a 200,000 name list, three best-selling books, a blog with more than one million monthly visitors, the title of lifehacker extraordinaire, and a number one book on the *New York Times*, *Wall Street Journal*, and *Business Week* bestsellers lists. Ah yes, and he also gets big fat checks regularly, which he collects from an exotic and remote destination of his choice.

Is Tim superior to the average human being?

Perhaps.

Does the message in his books break molds? Is it that well-written, captivating, educational?

Perhaps.

So then?

What's the secret behind his team's success?

Tim has a formula—a formula to market smarter, faster, and cheaper than everyone else.

The gist of that formula?

Simple. Tim markets around the product as opposed to the product itself.

Filing away traditional marketing techniques, Ferriss works inhumanly hard at promoting himself—the leader, the entrepreneur, the face—and his concept, his idea—lifestyle design—to endless forms of digital media outlets in a short but intensive span of time.

Interestingly, *The 4-Hour Workweek* was rejected by twenty-five publishers.

Twenty-five rejection letters would be enough to send anyone else into a serious state of depression.

Not Tim.

When finally, in 2007, Random House accepted his book, he decided to market it heavily through bloggers with whom he had created personal relationships.

That approach has today sold over 1,350,000 copies of *The 4-Hour Workweek*, has sent the book into international stardom, having been translated into thirty-five different languages, and has kept it on the *New York Times* bestseller list for four years on.

But that wasn't the end of Tim's success story.

For his second book, *The 4-Hour Body*, Tim gave away thousands of advanced copies just before it was published, and on December 14th, the day the book was launched, all the book recipients were sent an email marked "URGENT," asking them to spend thirty seconds writing a review. Many did. This was his most controversial tactic.

Call it devious, unusual, intelligent, suspicious, whatever you want— Tim ended up with a solid foundation of 200 positive reviews in the first week.

Then, in November 2012, came the icing on the cake, literally—*The 4-Hour Chef*, a book designed to be an encyclopedic guide to the skill of meta-learning. With a page count of 672, it looks somewhat intimidating. But in fact, Ferriss designed the book to be shared— each chapter and section is more like an ensemble of self-contained albums. They're epic thematics broken down into three-minute tracks. Very clever.

Matt Mason, from peer-to-peer file sharing platform BitTorrent, with whom Ferriss established a solid pre-launch partnership, de-scribes how this book-as-album strategy gives authors like Ferriss a significant advantage. The ability to release chapters as singles cre-ates a continuous news cycle during pre-launch promotion, and it encourages radio play. It also provides the flexibility to micro-target by using different chapters to reach and activate different readers. It's easier to mobilise micro-collectives of readers than it is to move one big mainstream bloc: "if you want everyone to read your book, let everyone read your book. Placing content within the BitTorrent ecosystem has the effect of sampling, radio play, or TV advertising. It's just at infinite scale," Matt explains.

To promote *The 4-Hour Chef*, Ferriss released the first chapter of his book, in addition to 680MB of behind-the-scenes content, on BitTorrent. This content was downloaded by over 2 million people:

- 293,936 people clicked on to the book's trailer on YouTube

- 327,555 people clicked on to the author's website

- 880,009 people clicked on to the book's Amazon page

BitTorrent users accounted for 20 percent of the book trailer's total YouTube views and were also the single largest bloc of visitors to the book's website (Source: bit.ly). BitTorrent helped the book sell over 250,000 copies, earning it a place on every major bestseller list.

The Foundation: How A Software Membership Site Did A $1 Million Launch

The Foundation—it started as an idea in Dane Maxwell's mind. A place where wannabe software entrepreneurs could hang out and learn how to start a software business. Twelve months later, he launched this idea to the tune of $1 million in revenue.

The premise of The Foundation is that most software developers build the software first, and then they try to sell it. What Dane teaches is the opposite. First find a problem that customers have, pre-sell the software solution, and then build it.

So how did this fairytale story come to life?

To find out, I interviewed Dane's business partner, Andy Drish. Andy was heavily involved throughout the entire campaign and shared some nuggets of gold with me.

One thing Andy and Dane did well was to be around the right people. To start with, they built a tremendous relationship with Andrew from Mixergy. Mixergy is a website where Entrepreneurs go to learn all the skills they need to run a successful business—the perfect target market for future Foundation customers.

After Dane was interviewed by Mixergy, it had a snowball effect and everything else fell into place from there. Andy also found that by putting the Foundation's students out to be interviewed, it was even more powerful than Dane's interviews because the students were the ones who did the hard yards, set up the businesses using The Foundation's process, and made the money. So the social proof was phenomenal. In fact, Andy says that 80 percent of their marketing was approaching top blogs and business sites, and asking to be interviewed.

So relationships matter.

What made the launch so cool?

One thing they did was spend a ridiculous amount of time on the video script. One hundred hours writing the introduction video on the squeeze page. That's two full weeks of work on one video. What would happen if you decided to do nothing else for two weeks and just worked on a single video for a squeeze page?

Was it worth the time? Hell, yes!

Andy and Dane's philosophy is to look where everyone else is zigging, and then zag. By spending so much time on the video, it guaranteed it would be awesome.

Here is the level of detail they went into. When they were writing the script, one would read the script out loud to potential entrepreneurs, and then the other would watch the audience to see when people lost interest. Anytime anyone lost interest, they would change the script to make it more engaging.

I mean, who does this? That much detail!

Well, it worked. A 40 percent opt-in rate and 52 percent engagement rate at the end of the eight-minute video.

A few other things that were interesting:

1. They recently launched a podcast, and now it is one of the top twenty-five podcasts in all of iTunes, getting thousands of downloads every day.

2. Some of their students are ex-Facebook and Microsoft employees!

3. They did a six-video launch sequence, five videos stocked full of content, and one sales video to top it off.

4. Launch day was actually a disaster! The merchant account reduced their limit on launch day, so Andy had to switch merchant accounts, and then it was still a mess because they couldn't access the funds for over six months. So important to choose a launch-friendly merchant. In Australia I can vouch that eWay and Pin Payments are both launch friendly. (I've used them both on big launches without a hitch.)

Roses Only—Unusual Marketing Strategies To Dominate The Flower Market

Roses Only is the number one brand for ordering flowers in Australia. In fact, when a Nielsen research study asked consumers, "Name a flower company," 93 percent of respondents named "Roses Only." The technical term for this is "umprompted brand awareness." Regardless, it's an amazing feat.

I was delighted to interview James Stevens, CEO of Roses Only, and we had a candid discussion on how he's grown the business and what his top marketing tricks were. I found that Roses Only has built this brand predominately through above the line advertising (mainly newspaper, radio, television, and magazines). However, Roses Only has adopted two strategies that are really unique and you could certainly implement these for your business.

1. Sponsoring charity organisations

James has donated flowers and gifts to thousands of charity events over the last fifteen years. What he found was that nearly every charity needs a lot of flowers to thank all the volunteers and special guests. The cost of those flowers can run into thousands of dollars per event for the charity, which then comes off the bottom line and doesn't get spent helping the needy people the charity is supporting.

So what James does is provide the flowers at no charge for the charity, as a contra sponsorship deal. The charity gets flowers to hand out to its special guests, and Roses Only gets many mentions and its roses go in the hands of Tier 1 people who help out with the charity events. The people who get the flowers are also likely to become future customers next time they need to buy flowers, and the positive cycle continues. When a Tier 1 or Celebrity is walking around with Roses Only flowers, it's fantastic for the brand.

2. Selling branded umbrellas

James also revealed in passing that the company has sold 150,000 Roses Only branded umbrellas over the last eighteen years. I had to do a double-take and make sure I wrote the number down correctly. 150,000 umbrellas? Really? No, that's not a misprint.

Before I get into the how, let me explain what that means. These are very high quality umbrellas; you'd probably pay $50 or more for them in the shops. So they are the kind of umbrellas you would be happy to carry around with you on a rainy day. This means that every time it rains, there are up to 150,000 people in Australia holding Roses Only advertising. Brilliant! You couldn't buy that kind of advertising space!

How did the company do this? Easy. To start with, they subsidised the cost of the umbrellas. So the initial cost price was $22, and they sold the umbrellas for $19.95. As the volumes increased, they were able to achieve a better cost price, which helped with margins. Now they bring in a container at a time from China.

Action exercise: What promotional products could work for your business? Maybe umbrellas don't work for your business, but think of other promotional products that could work—pens, USB disks, mouse pads, etc.

How To Create A Viral Email Campaign Using Your Existing List

Tzvi Balbin is an experienced digital marketer previously heading up online marketing at CatchOfTheDay, one of Australia's fastest growing online retailers. While doing research for this book, I've been on the lookout for unusual email marketing tactics. And Tzvi was extremely generous in sharing a case study of how he created a viral email campaign. Here's his write-up of how he managed to do this:

> Initially working with a client to improve their deliverability, I was doing some research into the ISPs that were represented in their marketing list.
>
> I asked the simple question, "What ISPs are our subscribers using?"
>
> To do this, I used a simple formula in Excel: by removing everything before the "@" symbol I got a list of every domain represented in my client's subscriber list. Here's the formula:

johnsmith@g-mail.com	=RIGHT(C1,LEN(C1)-FIND("@",C1)+1)	

Here's the result: a list of email addresses in one column and their associated domain in the other. My results looked a bit like this:

johnsmith@g-mail.com	g-mail.com	
moses@tablets.com	tablets.com	
big@data.com	data.com	

Using an advanced filter, I then did a count on each of the unique domains in the list before exporting the result and graphing it on two axes: X representing the domain name and Y showing the count for that domain. The result was similar to this graph:

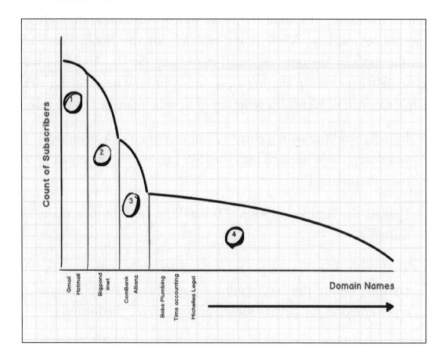

This is when things start to get interesting. You will notice that this graph looks similar to a long-tail search report: the majority of customers fell into obvious domains like @gmail.com or @live.com, but a huge portion fell into other, more specific domains. This got me wondering: How can I take over the world using that long tail?

That needs a little bit of investigating, Watson!

At scale the breakdown for most lists will be divided into four sections:

1. Major ISPs: Gmail, Hotmail, Yahoo

2. Smaller ISPs: Bigpond, iinet (these are Australian mid-size ISPs)

3. Big corporations with large head count: CommBank, J.P. Morgan, MinterEllison, Allianz Insurance, Wal-Mart, etc.

4. Small businesses: Bob's Plumbing, Tim's Accounting, those sorts of businesses

Buckets three and four are the true long tail here. This is where I discovered a golden opportunity for some unorthodox, personalized email marketing. What if I used the domain name that they subscribed with to personalize an email?

The Nuts And Bolts: What Tzvi Did

Using each of the domains in the list, I added a new column to our email marketing database called "company." For example, if I worked at Qantas, my email might be user@qantas.com and my "company" value would have the entry Qantas. If I worked at Coca-Cola and my email was user@coke.com, my company column would read Coke and so on.

We decided we were going to send out a "special offer" for each of these companies so we created a coupon code for every single company mentioned in the "company" column. My thought process was that customers at individual businesses and corporations would respond positively to a personalized coupon code: a code that looked like it was just for them. At work, people sit in close proximity. The idea was to exploit this phenomenon and get people to share and talk about the discount they had just received because they worked at Qantas.

I wanted to test the theory that they'd share this email within their place of work. The email we created used the dynamic coupon codes twice in the email: once in the subject line and once in the actual email. It was a bit like this:

Awesome…and kind of spooky! Picture this:

Rachel receives our email and leans over her cubicle to Matt.

Rachel: Did you get that discount from [insert your brand name]?

Matt: Nope, what's the discount?

Jimmy overhears.

Jimmy: It's a discount on [insert products here]. The code is [insert dynamic coupon], just head to domain.com to grab the deal.

Let the viral spread begin! In general, and especially at work, people feel validated when they share good information: It puts them in a position of "power" or "aloofness." As such, Rachel and Jimmy should be happy to share the personalized deal because it is a way of saying, "Without me, you wouldn't have received this discount." It's just human nature.

Show Me The Money: Measuring The Viral Effects

Next morning, I logged in to see how the campaign went.

It went really well. Christmas-came-early well!

Here are some results:

- Open Rates: increased by 32 percent over our regular statistics

- Click-through rates: increased by 55 percent over our regular statistics

- Average Order Value: increased by 13 percent over our regular statistics

- Conversion rates: up by 86 percent!

Google Analytics specifically measured the clicks and the associated revenues the email had generated…but I went a little further and ran a query on our database to display all of the transactions that had used one of the coupon codes from the email campaign. I discovered that the total revenue figures were approximately 35 percent higher than what Google Analytics was reporting.

Why?

Then it hit me: Database revenue minus Google Analytics revenue was essentially equal to the viral effect of our campaign—in cold hard cash. The difference represented those who hadn't received the email but whose colleagues told them about the discount. In most instances, Google Analytics recorded these customers as direct visits and attributed the revenue to that channel, while the people who actually received the email and clicked it had the revenue attributed to that correct email campaign tag.

An extra 35 percent revenue thanks to customers sharing your campaign? Yes, please!

On the back of this success, we started sending this campaign monthly. Even better, there might even have been a flow-on effect. Assume for a moment that many of the customers who ordered on that day got their products delivered to their workplace. After their orders are dispatched, not only do they arrive on the same day but all at the same time. Imagine you're at work and ten people get parcels, but you don't. You're bound to ask "What's going on?" And inevitably one of your colleagues will tell you "There are monthly discounts from [insert your company name] just for us. Subscribe with your work email and they will send you one."

Seriously Viral

The only downside to this style of campaign is that company email addresses have a higher attrition rate than personal emails: working for a company is generally not "forever" so you are naturally likely to lose some subscribers month-over-month, but the viral effects more than pay for this churn!

Strategic Media Buying—Getting Dirt Cheap Traffic To Your Site (That Also Converts)

Ben Simkin is a world class media buyer. He is consistently able to get great traffic at very affordable prices. I asked Ben to share some of his best advice on media buying and also to make it tangible by sharing some specific examples. Here's what he said:

> Media buy is an essential part of your campaign in order for you to generate more traffic and exposure; however, it must be approached strategically to ensure your campaign is successful.
>
> A common mistake we see marketers and business owners make is chasing the cheapest advertising and the cheapest clicks. This is a tactical way to approach your marketing, and tactics make up only a small part of a successful campaign.
>
> Before you even begin, your media buy campaign needs to start with profiling and understanding your target market. Without undertaking this critical process, your campaign will fail no matter how cheap you can get clicks for.
>
> Profiling your target market begins with defining their demographics, but not only their basic stats such as age, marital status, and location—more importantly, you need to define their psychographics.
>
> Psychographics are the personalities, values, interests, and lifestyles of your target market. Uncovering this information about your target market will allow you not only to communicate effectively with them through your marketing, but also discover the best way to reach them.

To illustrate what I mean, let's assume you are a golf swing instructor and you want to get more customers.

Now most people would find the best golfing websites, negotiate a deal, and run an advertising campaign on the top two golfing websites.

Now, there is nothing wrong with this, but let's look at an alternative strategy.

Let's assume you have performed extensive research on your target market, defined your demographics and psychographics, and discovered that most of your favourite clients are dentists and doctors.

These clients are the friendliest of all your different clients, they don't mind paying your fee, and they are just overall fun to be around. You decide you want more clients like these.

You research what websites dentists and doctors visit regularly and find a medical website aimed at doctors that also provides advertising opportunities.

It looks like the perfect opportunity.

So, what you decide to do is run a banner advertising campaign on this medical website targeted to doctors.

You find the advertising rates are a lot cheaper than the golfing websites, and you also find you are getting far better click-through rates because your golfing banner stands out on this website which is primarily made up of bland articles about medical procedures.

If you had advertised on the golfing websites, the obvious choice, your banner ads, would have been lost in the noise of competing offers and similar colour schemes.

Your click-through rates would be average, and as a result, your success would be limited.

All the other local golf swing instructors are still investing heavily on the golfing websites, trying to compete head-to-head with each other, while you stay "under the radar" and steal all the clients away for yourself. This all happened because you thought about your marketing strategically.

Leveraging Your Media Buying Results By Remarketing

Media buy can be quite expensive when compared to other traffic sources, so one thing you need to learn to do is how to leverage your ad spend to maximise your results.

One way to do this is with remarketing.

Remarketing lets you show ads to users who've previously visited your website as they browse the Web.

Well now that you have website visitors who all match your ideal client, you can start to build an audience with these highly targeted visitors and advertise to them on cheaper platforms, such as Facebook.

So while you may spend $4 for a click-through Media Buy, you can get clicks on Facebook as cheap as a few cents.

Using the same example of the golf swing instructor, you start to collect an audience of doctors whom you can now target specifically through Facebook for a much cheaper price.

And not only targeting that audience, but also their friends who are most likely going to be in the same profession too. Because let's face it, doctors generally hang around doctors.

So if you are getting clicks for $4 and clicks for 10 cents, what this will do is lower your cost-per-click average overall and allow you to achieve more conversions for a lower price.

This strategy also provides many more advantages, such as reinforcing your marketing message on various platforms, allowing you to create tailored messages to your target audience and test multiple offers to see which ones convert the best.

How A Landscaper Got 100 Qualified Leads For Less Than $4,000

We had a client, Nick, in the landscape design business, so what we did, as we normally do, was analyse his current business and specifically his target market.

We went through his client list over the last few years and discovered that most of his clients who wanted landscape design were successful business owners. But one curious thing to note was they were never the ones who requested the quotes. It turns out it was usually the wife of the business owner who asked for a landscape design quote.

So that gave us some information to start working out his targeting. We knew we should target women, but we didn't have enough information yet to make sure the marketing would be successful.

When speaking to Nick about his clients, he described the wives as well-dressed women, which led us to understand they were fashion conscious and had a passion for high-end clothes and accessories.

We needed then to think about what types of websites his target client visited frequently.

So we went about coming up with an extensive list of fashion blogs. We had quite a long list, but we needed to find out which ones would enable us to advertise geographically. We only wanted to target Sydney because that was his serviceable area.

We found three blogs that allowed us to advertise to Sydney residents.

The blog owners also confirmed with us that their website visitors were affluent women. We knew we were onto a good thing.

We were able to secure an excellent price, cheaper than any media buy website we have come across before or since.

Meanwhile, all of Nick's competitors were using expensive and overcrowded advertising platforms, trying to fight over the same group of clientele.

Our strategy was, rather than try and get them to request a quote straight away, we would build up a database of women in Sydney, who liked fashion and had an interest in garden designs. These were his ideal client types.

We offered a free guide on the Top 10 Garden Designs in Sydney as an incentive for them to sign up.

From there, with our mailing list, not only did we provide valuable and visual emails to keep the readers engaged, but we also offered a Free Landscape Design Consult.

Nick was able to generate 100 quotes over the next four months and spent less than $4,000 in advertising.

Rather than going through Google Display Network, approach the Blog Owner directly, and negotiate a deal—chances are it will be a lot cheaper than Google, and the blog owner will make more $ because he or she is getting paid directly. Our email to the blog owner was:

Dear (Blog Owner),

I am a regular reader of your blog and I have noticed you have Google ads running on your blog.

I am a business owner and I have a product that would align with your readers' interests, so I was wondering if we could come to an arrangement whereby I can place a banner on your blog (where the Google one is now) and pay you directly? The benefit for you is you cut out the middle-man and get paid more; for me, the benefit is I can offer my product to your readers and get more clients.

If you are interested, I would like to talk to you further.

Regards,

Ben

Action Exercise: Approach a blogger who looks like he or she could do with some revenue. See if the blogger will do a media buy deal with you and you'll be pleasantly surprised with the results!

13

WANT TO DO THIS STUFF
FOR COMPANIES?

*"My greatest strength as a consultant is to be
ignorant and ask a few questions."*
— **Peter Drucker**

You can take all the strategies in this book and use them for your
current employer or in your own business. But what if your current
business isn't keen on these ideas? You can then offer to do these
strategies as a consultant for other businesses.

If you don't want to leave your current job, you can do these strategies before or after work, or on weekends. It's the Internet. As long as
you have a phone and computer, you can do any of these techniques.
In fact, I would recommend staying in your current job until you are
either earning enough online to replace your income, or you get a job
in marketing that you love.

This chapter isn't long because it doesn't need to be. I could give
you 1,000 templates, phone scripts, direct mail letters, fancy business
cards, and whatever to get consulting gigs. None of that is going to
make one shred of difference.

If you want to become a marketing consultant to businesses, it is really easy. You just have to make a decision to do it. As Henry Ford famously said, "Whether you think you can, or you think you can't—you're right."

I know it sounds too simple to be true, but it actually is that easy. There are a million books out there on consulting and how to get consulting gigs. These books have some good info, but they'll make it unnecessarily complicated.

Here's the order I would approach it in if I were starting from scratch:

You Can Do Your First Job For Free As A Trial

Just say to a business owner or marketing director, "Hey, I've learnt these great skills from this book, and I need a business to test them out with; can I try them out on your business?" Most businesses are going to be delighted to have you try out innovative new marketing strategies for them that won't cost them anything to implement.

Here's the thing. Once you get someone to say, "Yes" to this proposition, this is what you need to do. Read this very closely. Treat this as if you are being paid $1 million to do this campaign. Treat it as if it were your own business. If you're doing this full time, get there early, stay late, offer to do any tasks that come along.

Then get started on all of the strategies you've learnt in this book. If they've got no list and no budget, then do the "bare-bones" launch you learnt about in Chapter 2. If you can get some revenue in the door for them while you're on trial, and it didn't cost them any money, they will be doing back flips!

If they've got a small budget, then choose the strategies in this book that make the most sense.

If they've got a large budget, then hire an army of marketers and you can manage them.

This is what normally happens when someone approaches me for a free trial. I generally accept his offer if he appears to have the right attitude. And then he starts off well on Day 1. Then as the days go by, the person generally gets worse and worse.

He doesn't try that hard because he's not getting paid. He'll get there late and leave early. He'll call in sick. He'll do a "half-job" and I'll be left to clean up his unfinished work. It's very rare to get someone with the right attitude who turns up for a trial.

Although it's not all doom and gloom. I've seen it happen a couple of times at E-Web, where someone has come in for a trial, and he has impressed us so much that we've offered him a permanent paid role in the company. It's so easy to stand out from the crowd; just put in the extra 10 percent that the average person doesn't do!

Charge A Consulting Fee For Your Time

This one sounds good, but it is tricky to get right, especially if you're a newbie. You can charge an hourly rate or a fixed fee for a certain amount of work. I'm a fan of a fixed fee for an agreed scope of work. The challenge is that the scope can always change.

One of my first consulting gigs was doing some work for a guy who was selling "driver fatigue alarms." What's a driver fatigue alarm? Great question. It's like an earpiece that detects whether you're falling asleep at the wheel while you are driving. A great device. Saves lives. Brilliant for truck drivers. The only problem is it's really hard to sell!

People don't wake up in the morning and think to themselves "I need a driver fatigue alarm." So it's a "push sell." You've got to create the demand by putting advertising in front of the right people. It's what I call "educating the market."

Educating the market is great if you're Microsoft and have a billion dollar budget, but when you're a small business, it's just not going to work.

How does all of this relate to consulting?

Well, when I took on the driver fatigue alarm gig, I agreed to do part-time work for $1,500/month. I thought part-time would mean maybe one day a week, and then I would have the rest of the week to work on other consulting projects and pick up higher paying clients.

I thought wrong.

Part-time turned out to be basically full-time. Because it was so hard to sell the product, I felt obliged to put in more hours to help get more sales in. I'm the kind of person who takes on every project like it's my own business, regardless of how much or how little I get paid.

After the first month, the company and I parted ways amicably, and thankfully, I picked up a few other consulting gigs straight after.

The reason why I shared that story is to show you that you shouldn't cut yourself short. I know this sounds ironic because I just told you to work for free, but this is different. You charge a consulting fee once you have at least one reference on board and you have proved yourself as a marketer. And once you have proved yourself as a marketer, you need to get paid as a marketer. If your fee is too low, you won't feel motivated to do the job right.

If you're good at your job and you can deliver results that exceed the consulting fee you are charging, then you won't have any problem finding work.

You Can Charge A Lower Fee For Your Time + A Percentage Of Sales

This is another tricky one to get right. You'd only do this if you felt like the business was a "slam dunk." Here's my criteria for a slam dunk—

it has been influenced by my friend Alexi Neocleous' thoughts as well as my practical experience of what's easy or hard:

1. Product is already created and is selling in the market—ideally it's digital so the margins are there.

2. Client has good credibility—ideally he has had some media exposure...some level of profile already built.

3. An internal list—minimum of 5,000, but ideally more. It's not much, I know. But if they have a good relationship, great. Even better if they are buyers.

4. Social media—a few thousand fans would be nice, as a starting point.

5. A back end higher-priced product already in place.

6. Basic understanding of selling and Internet marketing.

7. Their core pain point is execution—so from an emotive perspective they *want* to hit it out of the park, but they know that they just can't pull resources together.

8. You are given authority to make decisions and execute marketing strategies within a framework.

Super-Advanced Strategy

You can offer to join the business as a business partner and get equity in the business in return for doing the marketing work. At E-Web, we've done a few of these deals and they're brilliant. Both your and the client's interests are aligned because you are business partners. The only downfall is that these are expensive to setup (you need to register a new company, and sign shareholder agreements, get bank accounts, arrange for finances, etc.). And it's extremely important to make sure you share the same values as the business partner, so you agree on the strategy and the business' direction.

Done well, you and the business partner can both be very successful out of this type of agreement. Only attempt to form one of these partnerships once you've already done some good consulting work for other people.

And you're now at the end of the book. Well done for getting here. Most people who buy marketing books don't read them. Most people who read marketing books don't take action. Most people who take action try it once, fail, and never try it again.

Don't be like most people. You're better than that.

The strategies in this book have made people millions and millions of dollars. You've got to give them a try. You've come this far.

Enough reading and time for one last action exercise.

Action Exercise: Get out there and start implementing what you've learnt in this book. If you've got no experience, start with a free trial. Which strategy are you going to use to start getting some consulting work?

FREE BOOK RESOURCES PAGE

Some of the content couldn't fit in these pages, so I have collated it all in a free book resources page!

Visit http://www.feedastarvingcrowd.com/resources to download:

- Screenshots of successful campaigns

- Actual results of high-performing marketing campaigns (including advertising copy, cost-per-clicks, and conversion rates)

- Webpage wireframes you can use for your own website that are proven to convert

- Diagrams and flow charts of automated marketing sequences that have been responsible for millions of dollars of sales

- Links to websites that have world class sales copywriting and are converting truckloads of visitors to buyers

- Interviews (media files and transcripts) with other marketing experts

- Links to online platforms where you can find other people to promote your product

To get all of this content, just go to:
http://www.feedastarvingcrowd.com/resources

ABOUT THE AUTHOR

Robert Coorey, MBA, is a #1 best-selling author and wildly successful marketer. Currently, he's Director of Global Business at E-Web Marketing, Australia's top online marketing agency. He's obsessed with helping others achieve unheard of results through innovative strategies to feed starving crowds of buyers. Robert is actively driving a world-record webinar attempt.

Robert has an MBA from Macquarie Graduate School of Management and a Bachelor of Computer Science from Macquarie University.

ABOUT E-WEB MARKETING

With over fourteen years of online marketing experience and hundreds of satisfied clients, E-Web Marketing is here to make the Internet a better, happier, and more profitable place for Australian businesses. *E-Web Marketing exists to bring Happiness, Success, and Fun to everyone we encounter.*

E-Web Marketing has won the Deloitte technology Fast 50 award for five years straight, been in the Top 10 places to work in Australia for three years running, and in the BRW fastest 100 growing companies in Australia.